150—strong

150-Strong

A Pathway
to a Different Future

Rob O'Grady

150-Strong:
A Pathway to a Different Future

© 2016 Rob O'Grady

Cover art: Ken Avidor

Publication date: January 24, 2016

ISBN-13: 978-1523676521
ISBN-10: 1523676523

Club Orlov Press
http://ClubOrlovPress.blogspot.com
cluborlovpress@gmail.com

Introduction

This book is the happy end of a longish story.

In early 2013 I was invited to speak at the North House Folk School in Grand Marais, Minnesota. It is a school that teaches a wide variety of native and folk arts, from building canoes to baking bread. One of the things that this school does rather well is teach people how to become part of the community that has grown up around the school. This had been happening spontaneously for some time, and it was thought that a conscious effort in this direction would produce even better results. And so, I was invited to address this topic in a seminar.

This was a new topic for me, and so I spent a few weeks at the library researching small communities that have stood the test of time. I looked at a great many of them: religious communities, such as the Anabaptists—the Amish, Mennonites and Hutterites, as well as the Mormons in Utah and the Dukhobors in British Columbia; secular ones, such as the Kibbutzim in Israel; ethnically defined ones such as the Roma (also called Gypsies) and the Pashtun tribesmen of Afghanistan and Pakistan.

My criteria were simple: I looked at small communities that had stood the test of time—a century at least, ideally longer. What I was looking for was not their particulars (although I found them engrossing) but their commonalities. This was as diverse a set as could be imagined, defying any attempt to categorize: religious and secular, liberal and conservative, settled and nomadic, pacifist and warlike, isolationist and cosmopolitan, with different and similar roles for men and women, with and without private property, with and without a formal authority, with and without written law, democratic and authoritarian... and yet in spite of all these differences a consistent picture emerged: all of them exhibited a certain set of common traits.

Amazed by my discoveries, I presented my findings, first at the North House Folk School, and a few weeks later at the "Age of Limits" Conference at the Four Quarters Interfaith Sanctuary in Pennsylvania. While the audience at the school was very receptive and attentive, and used my presentation to jump-start a very serious set of discussions, the audience at the conference rose up in rebellion. You see, none of the communities I described as exemplifying the common set of successful traits was acceptable to every part of the audience: they were either too much of one thing, or too little of something else.

A particular sticking point was the lack of gender equality in almost all of them (the Kibbutzim were the one exception). Their lack of gender equality is not the least bit surprising, given that most of these communities were founded (and became set in their ways) a long time ago—which was the reason I thought they were worth a look. Back then "gender" was strictly a grammatical term, while the ideal of *égalité* was yet to be proclaimed by the French revolutionaries. Nevertheless, I was loudly criticized for holding up such retrograde communities as examples.

Since I was not interested in specifics and peculiarities, but in generalities and commonalities, I put this criticism down to certain people's inability to see the forest for the trees, and went on to publish a collection of articles on the topic, titled *Communities that Abide*[1]. In it I laid out my case, supplemented by a number of articles along similar lines by some quite illustrious contributors. In it, I distilled the set of traits that I thought were responsible for the ability of these communities to abide to "thirteen commandments," which I playfully cast in the same form as the commandments of Pastafarianism, a.k.a. the Church of the Flying Spaghetti Monster: "You probably shouldn't..." in place of "Thou shalt not..."

Although *Communities that Abide* sold out the initial print run and has continued to sell quite well ever since, it has left something to be desired. It's an interesting little book, but as an organizational tool it has turned out to be quite useless. You see, it's not just a matter of not seeing the forest for the trees—it's more a question of there being a forest in place of an open meadow. What's needed is not a set of recommendations (or commandments, however playfully expressed) but a set of **first principles**. People want to be able to think things through on their own, and come up with their own recommendations. People don't want to just apply a recipe, no matter how scrupulously and impartially it was formulated.

And now... the happy ending. Into the breach steps Rob O'Grady. He had read and was inspired by *Communities that Abide,* as had many others, but what he then did with it was nontrivial and unique. He took the basic message of *Communities that Abide*, stripped it of every bit of extraneous detail, and then built up the case from the ground up, based on first principles.

He explains the urgency with which society needs to be reorganized should we wish to leave to our children a pleasant and surviv-

---

1 http://amazon.com/dp/1500742929/

able world. He explains why none of the existing large-scale systems of social control—be they capitalist or communist—would work. He lays out the basic requirements that must be fulfilled in order for a community to function well. He explains the basic principle—the **reconciling principle**—which can resolve conflicts as they arise. This principle cannot be based on selfishness (a.k.a. the profit motive). Also, it cannot be impersonal: it can only operate *if we personally know* every other person. This limits the maximum size of the community to Dunbar's Number—around 150 individuals.

Rob manages to do all this without introducing any cultural, religious or ideological specifics. His text is so ecumenical that it is not even specifically Christian—or based on any other religion, other than a spiritual bond with our living planet—the only one we will ever know—that is universally human. His writing appeals not to any culture, class, tribe, group or party, but directly to *human nature*.

These are weighty matters, but Rob's book is not a scientific treatise on the problematics of social organization: it is a textbook suitable for an introductory course. But it is also a guide that contains a call to action; not any specific set of actions—that is left entirely up to you—but perfectly general action that will bring you together with the 150 people who are closest to you in a way that will make each one of us 150-strong.

Dmitry Orlov
January 2016
Beaufort, South Carolina

Table of Contents

Prologue

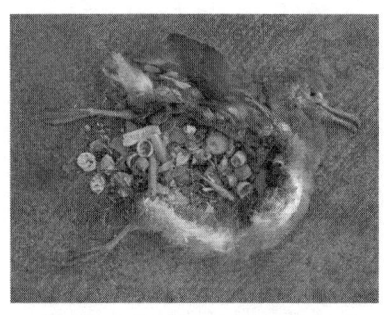

Albatross Chick on Midway Island

In the center of the Pacific Ocean, hundreds of miles from the mainland, the shores of Midway Island are scattered with the carcasses of dead albatross chicks that lie decomposing, revealing stomachs full of plastic debris—items washed into the sea and unintentionally inserted in to the marine food chain. The plight of these seabirds symbolizes humankind's collective disregard for the Earth.

The majority of us have become inured to such degradation, and assimilate the fact that we are the perpetrators of the 6th mass extinction event evident in the Earth's geologic record with only minor discomfort. Our governments lack the

1

wherewithal to frame the problem in a meaningful way, let alone do anything about it, and the prevailing approach of the general population is little better, mostly limited in scope to token efforts in areas such as recycling and the maintenance of good intentions.

Given that the response to such challenges is so woefully ineffective, the question that is presented is: Do we have the capacity to do things differently? To reverse the process by which we are turning our planet into a "pile of filth" as Pope Francis recently suggested?

The backdrop to the unfolding of this calamity is an economic system that seems to be driving us ever further toward some point of criticality. Whenever environmental problems are discussed at a political level, solutions are sought within the confines of our existing economic arrangements, with the overriding concern that environmental protection measures should not adversely affect economic growth. But it has long been obvious that this very concern is the reason why measures implemented to address environmental damage fall short.

Pope Francis

The current economic system is also characterized by increasing levels of inequality and alienation that seem to be driving us farther away from a point of social equilibrium. This situation is poignantly illustrated by the Antilia Building in Mumbai, India, which is a $1 billion, 27-story home for just one family. It has a 3-story ballroom, a staff of 600, a six-level garage and 3 helicopter pads. It also comes with a great view of the Dharavi slum where, through the smog, over half a million people can be seen living with almost nothing. There, the population density is 1 person per 4m^2 and they have one toilet per 1,440 residents. There are no reported ballrooms or helicopter pads.

This system has a brutalizing effect on the general population. New Zealand, the country where I live, is relatively prosperous, safe and unspoiled, but more than 1 in 10 people here is prescribed antidepressants. Many more medicate themselves with alcohol and narcotics.

We are all busy negotiating life's joys, sorrows, triumphs and hurdles, and generally attempting to make the best of whatever situation we find ourselves in. In approaching the challenges that are presented, few of us realize that we are actively engaged in environmental destruction or contributing to the economic misfortune of others. The narratives of our culture fail to join the dots for us, and a realistic assessment of where we are and what we need to do is beyond the comprehension of most.

The Antilla Building

Our challenge is therefore to reconcile the status quo—the context of our everyday lives as householders, employers and employees, parents, sons, daughters, students and citizens—with the big picture issues in a way that would make sense of it all, and give us an inkling of what we might be able to do about it.

Author's Note

This book began as a response to the use of the word "sustain-ability," a concept I became connected to through my training in sustainability engineering: the design and incorporation of environmentally-friendly practices into commerce and indus-try. It is based on principles such as these:

• When one cuts down a tree, plant a new one.

• We should try to use the waste from one process as a re-source for another.

• Polluters should bear the costs of their actions.

All of these seem like good and logical ideas. But there is a rather significant problem in attempting to work in this way, because the greater context in which such efforts are cur-rently being made reduces them to a farce: our current system of economics, which encourages short term accumulation of financial profit, is fundamentally incompatible with sustainability. This, to use a colorful colloquialism, makes such efforts akin to "farting against thunder."

That is not to say that profit is inherently a negative thing. The creation of a financial surplus, in its most earnest expression, could be equated with prudent and efficient house-holding. But if nature is to serve as our model, then we can see something of how our current approach to profit has become problematic.

The accumulation of a surplus is a natural process: a plant accumulates surplus energy and nutrients to be able to bear fruit; a polar bear accumulates a surplus in the form of body fat which enables it to survive the winter; and our hunter-gatherer ancestors collected a surplus of food so that they would be able to survive in lean times. But in the monomaniacal pursuit of profit that we are engaged in at present, there is little that is natural about it, little sensitivity to the intricacies of the environmental and social systems that sustain us.

The reason for this can be deduced from a simple formula:

$$Profit = Income - Expenses$$

From it we can see that the profit motive and the "sustainability motive" are diametrically opposed: If sustainability initiatives were to truly succeed beyond the narrow realms of such things as waste minimization and embracing new technology, they would result in less income (due to reduced consumption) and more expenses (due to the cost of mitigation measures) leading to lower profits.

This inverse relationship between profit and sustainability is hugely important, and it is the proper starting point in any effort to confront our large-scale environmental problems. Yet it is almost universally ignored in official circles, and political efforts to address sustainability issues give it almost no coverage.

The position of ignorance which our elected leaders maintain with regard to the incompatibility of our system of economics with sustainability is but one example of the human tendency toward delusion—an unfortunate condition that is common to us all.

One interested observer of this particular psychological flaw is the billionaire investor Charlie Munger, a partner of Warren Buffet, a previous holder of the title of the world's richest man. Munger has

Charlie Munger

made his fortune by trying to eliminate his tendencies toward delusion. Audiences are captivated by him when he shares his common-sense pearls of wisdom. In a 1995 Harvard lecture on "the psychology of human misjudgment" he described 24 standard causes of irrational decision-making, prominent among which is "incentive-caused bias." Put simply, it is incentives that shape human behavior, and if one knows what the operative incentive structure is, one can be reasonably sure about what the outcome will be. Since our economic system is centered around profit, the accumulation of which aligns with more consumption and less expenditure on environmental protection, sustainability can only be an afterthought—a luxury we can afford when profits are plentiful.

In our current way of doing things, the conflict between profit and sustainability is resolved through regulation, where all must comply with certain rules that hurt profitability a little bit but avoid worse damage. And, indeed, this approach has produced many good outcomes: the air is cleaner in Los Angeles, the fish are returning to River Thames, and many large areas of undeveloped land have been protected as national parks. But, for many reasons, it is an approach that is flawed: it doesn't handle complexity well; it breaks down when there are different laws in different countries; and it only works when there is a social context in which the law is supported and enforced.

As soon as one tries to address these problems, sustainability becomes an unapproachable subject: to address it at the

Naomi Klein

big-picture level one has to address the underlying economic and social context, but that is something of a taboo. Nevertheless, there is some mainstream discussion opening up on this topic, including some positive response to Naomi Klein's book, *This Changes Everything: Capitalism vs. The Climate* (2014), and increasingly, it seems, the need to consider alternatives to our current system is being recognized.

What follows is my attempt to contribute to this discussion. Though I give the word "sustainability" only a passing mention, it is the prism through which I view our predicament. I believe that it is only by critically examining the structure of our current economic system, and by exploring how things could be done differently, that a scenario for a more sustainable future can be explored.

The title of Naomi Klein's book provides a useful segue into the opening chapter: I feel that it is not quite correct to frame our current situation in terms of a conflict between Capitalism and Climate (or any other sustainability issue). The current iteration of capitalism needs no opponent. It is critically deteriorating by itself, due to its implicit structural flaws.

The demise of capitalism has long been predicted by many —those who have understood the nature of its flaws—but it just hasn't happened yet. But sooner or later the confluence of favorable conditions and delaying tactics, which have forestalled the inevitable terminal crisis of capitalism, will run their course. As the aftermath of the "Global Financial Crisis" of 2008 has demonstrated, that which is unsustainable cannot be sustained forever, and before too long inevitable outcomes do eventually come to pass.

1. Taking Stock

In the ebb and flow of nature things usually occur in cycles.

Our sun, the life-giving force of our Solar System, is a con-glomeration of elements, born of the effects of gravity, which pulled together dust and gas from the vastness of space into a tight mass. The temperature and pressure generated by this process eventually jump-started a nuclear fusion reaction that continues to this day, generating light and heat that sustain us here on Earth.

And just as the sun came into being in a process of cosmic genesis, one day it shall cease to be; scientists speculate that it will eventually expand out into the Solar System, taking the form of a red giant, engulfing the Earth, before fizzling out to become a white dwarf, a residual mass with most of its energy spent.

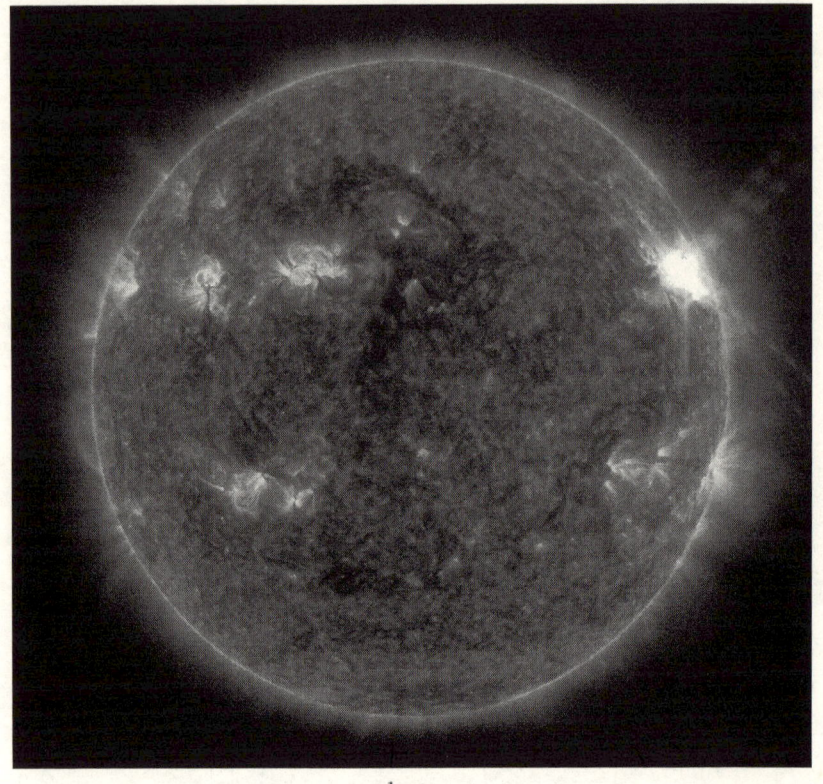

The Sun

On this scale we can see that our pithy human existence is insignificant and transitory, and that on all scales, large and small, always there is change and renewal. One season passes into another, death is the companion of life, and the only constant is that things never stay the same.

And as we reflect on our current situation, stepping back to take a big picture view beyond the machinations of our daily lives, it would seem that a period of change is close ahead for homo sapiens in our short sojourn as the dominant species on planet Earth. The days of plenty that have sustained our recent summer of materialistic expansion, resplendent with a ripe abundance of resources and an ever-expanding population, are coming to an end, and the autumn of consolidation is upon us.

The cycle of growth

In the natural sciences, the life-cycle of populations can be represented by a "logistic curve," which is used to characterize the cycle of growth of a system bounded by external limits. An emergent population, once established, grows rapidly until it starts to impinge upon the carrying capacity of its environment, but then comes a shock point beyond which it can grow no more.

As inhabitants of a planet that is finite in size, we too are subject to the humbling reality of the logistic curve, although it would seem that we are largely ignoring it at present. Our current mode of living, which harnesses roughly 1.5 times the Earth's biological productive capacity, depleting nonrenewable resources at an astoundingly reckless rate, is no doubt putting significant and unsustainable stresses on the systems that sustain us, socially, economically and environmentally, and these stresses must eventually have consequences.

In terms of where this places us, three things can happen:

1. The limits to growth can be removed by some change to the system, resulting in the growth curve on the graph shooting up again.

2. Some sort of self-regulating equilibrium can be established, resulting in the curve flattening out to a steady-state wobble.

3. There is a crash, which is what usually happens when a system overshoots its natural limits.

What awaits us we cannot know, but we can be sure that there are interesting times ahead.

The maxim "show me the incentive and I will show you the outcome" provides a bite-sized introduction to what follows in this book. Its main premise is that the incentive structure that we currently operate by is surely directing us toward a point of inevitable decline, such that we shall go the way of the Romans, Aztecs, Babylonians and every other civilization that has fallen before ours.

The main message of this book is that we are blind to the significance of the **reconciling force** of our current system, which happens to be inherently negative, and that it is only by understanding this that we may have some chance of finding a better way of doing things, for anything else would be but tinkering around the edges.

In seeking to provide a bridge to something better, a very successful and proven system that operates with an alternative, positive reconciling force is examined. It is based on Dunbar's number, which originates in evolutionary biology and proposes an upper limit to the number of people that humans can maintain effective social relationships with, which is approximately 150 people.

The significance of Dunbar's number is that it delineates a threshold above which patterns of human interaction change from personal to impersonal. At present, almost all our systems of societal organization involve groups of more than 150 people, and are therefore impersonal. Scale is the enemy of personal attention and thoughtfulness, and one of the consequences of this prevailing state of depersonalization is that it has dulled our ability to respond to the challenges we face on an appropriate level.

In seeking solutions, history and precedent are always a useful place to start. Looking into the past, we can see that our current swing toward impersonal arrangements is an aberration. For most of human history we lived in groups sized roughly in accordance with Dunbar's number, in villages, clans, tribes and communities. In this context personal relationships are the most important system of regulation, and this creates a very different dynamic from what we are experiencing in the present day.

But before presenting the details of where this analysis might lead us, it is first necessary to take stock of our current situation, and to understand what has brought us to this point.

Our economic system

On the surface, young people in the world's developed economies are presented with a world that is richer and more advanced than that which was bestowed on their parents and grandparents. But underneath that world is unstable.

Our financial system is essentially a faith-based system: our belief in the value of money and the structures that underpin it is what keeps the economic bubble that it sustains from popping. But this faith rests on increasingly shaky ground, as the central banks of the world—the ones who are charged with maintaining the integrity of money—are throwing out the rule book according to which the system has been maintained, and resorting to reckless experimentation in an effort to keep the bubble inflated. While they are managing to hold it together for the time being, this is but a grace period that will be inevitably followed by a period of negative outcomes.

The financial system is saturated with debt that is impossible to repay, and manipulated by wealthy interests that are only looking out for themselves: a situation that has left governments with no other option but to resort to the artificial stimulation of more and more debt creation. It is only this that allows the charade of solvency of the financial industry to continue. Ironically, more debt is what is now required to keep the system afloat, even though too much debt was the cause of the problem in the first place.

The ordinary person knows very little about how this is done, or even that it is occurring in the first place, because the methodology of reckless debt creation is disguised by various methods of financial chicanery that carry euphemistic acronyms such as QE, LTRO or POMO.[2] Nor does the ordinary person seem to care too much about it, so long as goods keep arriving at the stores and their wages keep getting paid. But eventually everyone will have to understand more. Finance is a system of equations and numbers; suspension of disbelief only gets you so far, and in the end the laws of mathematics must be obeyed.

The mathematical root of the problem is that, in a world where money is created as debt,[3] and where in any loan contract the loan principal is always less than the loan principal plus interest ($P < P + I$), it is fundamentally impossible for all

---

2 These are decoded as Quantitative Easing, Long-Term Refinancing Operation and Permanent Open Market Operations.

3 If the reader is unfamiliar with this problem there are several good explanatory clips on YouTube. Search for "Money as Debt."

debts to be repaid. The money required to repay the interest on debt does not exist until it is borrowed into existence, and debt must therefore expand continuously just to keep the system going. And while this can work for a long time, given a growing economy, where the value of assets appreciates according to their future earning potential, and the value of the collateral available in the system to facilitate more debt creation increases, it is a system that cannot last forever. In a world where there are limits to growth, such as an aging or contracting population, or where there are limited natural resources, the value of collateral for future borrowing cannot increase exponentially.

Eventually, when economic growth cannot keep up with the requirement of creating of ever more money to service the interest on the debt, the scheme will fail—no doubt about it. Anyone with a basic knowledge of mathematics can work that out. And when we find ourselves at the point we are at now, where new debt is created using the same collateral several times over (known as rehypothecation - similar to borrowing money against your house many times over from different banks), or where new debt is created using collateral that is worth nothing, such as a bundled-up package of "subprime" (i.e., bad) loans, or the sovereign debts of any one of a number of European nations, we know that this point is not too far off.

It is only a matter of time before this scheme will fail, with two scenarios being possible. In the first, new debt "stimulus" is brought into existence without any limits. Such artificial creation of new money can, for a period, keep things going. This is effectively a form of money printing—a debasing of the currency—which, in the end, with 100 percent certainty, results in hyperinflation, where money ceases to have any value beyond that of bits of colored plastic and paper with pictures and numbers on them. This has happened numerous times, most recently in 2009 in Zimbabwe. The same process is currently running its course in the Ukraine, in Kazakhstan and in Venezuela. This is the path that is currently being taken.

Zimbabwe: One Hundred Trillion Dollar Note

In the second scenario, the creation of new money is allowed to lag behind the amount required for servicing the interest on the existing debt, causing an economic depression, with large systemic bankruptcies in which huge chunks of debt are wiped out. The problem with this is that any single large bankruptcy of a "systemically important" (financial) institution, if it is allowed to happen, will cause a cascading sequence of defaults on an international scale, which will largely destroy most relationships based on money in what is known as a deflationary collapse.[4] This is what we observed in 2008 when the collapse of just one firm—Lehman Brothers—

_____

4 This will happen because of the interwoven web of counterparty risk that is the derivatives market.

brought about the sudden onset of a global financial crisis, in which the world came close to a "system collapse," in the words of then-US Treasury Secretary Hank Paulson.

And while in 2007-2008 it was possible to avoid serious problems through state intervention—through a proxy-state subsidy of banks[5] and the implicit government underwriting of all large bank debts—it is unlikely that such desperate measures would work again. Government bailouts for financial institutions who employ staff to gamble with

Hank Paulson

other people's money (considered such a skilled activity that it elevates them to a pay grade far beyond everyone else) are unlikely to be palatable to the everyday person the second time around. Such measures would be especially unpopular when accompanied by the line that further austerity and confiscation of ordinary citizens' bank deposits is necessary to pay for such largesse.

The idea that governments can run up debts endlessly, spending what they borrow to compensate for deficiencies in the real economy, without this ever causing a problem, is also

---

5 Through the facilitation of favorable relationships with central banks.

a fallacy. While all the new money produced through this method so far has not yet given rise to major inflation or a currency crisis, it is only a matter of time. The rule that debt must be repaid at some point needs to be maintained, or the whole system slides ever farther toward fantasy. Evidence of this was recently provided by Haruhiko Kuroda, Governor of the Bank of Japan, when he said this of his country's efforts to resolve its economic problems by ever more money printing:

"I trust that many of you are familiar with the story of Peter Pan, in which it says, 'the moment you doubt whether you can fly, you cease forever to be able to do it.'"

Eventually Mr. Kuroda and his central banker colleagues will be summoned back from Neverland and simple arithmetic will trump analogies from fairy stories.

Haruko Kuroda

There is also another growing problem. The capitalist model relies on the ability to evaluate risk in order to allocate capital efficiently. With risk artificially removed from the most important parts of the financial system, the financial industry has become an outsized monster that is continuously gorging itself on ever-cheaper money while starving the increasingly risky nonfinancial sectors of the economy of the actual goods and services which it is supposed to finance. At this point, feeding the financial sector more free money will simply make it even bigger and the problems of the real economy even worse. But not feeding it enough will cause everyone to suddenly see how risky the whole debt pyramid has become and to stampede toward the exits, causing financial markets to seize up.

Honest work has been hijacked by the financial class

In the meantime, one of the consequences of the intervention-ist actions being taken to prop up the financial system is that the gap in wealth between the very rich and everyone else is increasing rapidly. The richest 62 people in the world have as much as the poorest 3,500,000,000—a statistic that is stagger-ing in the extreme. What drives this rapid increase is the sim-ple fact that ordinary people do not have access to central bank credit at 0% interest like the financial class. They can only participate on the periphery of the speculative scheme that sustains the modern version of our debt-based economic system, where the risk is high and the pickings are slim, while the financial class can invest with relative impunity, safe in the knowledge that their bets are backstopped and underwrit-ten by powerful economic institutions, allowing them to accu-mulate ever more assets with relatively low risk.

In the new, manipulated economic world, the ordinary person cannot accumulate wealth through savings from wages or salary, or by working as an honest trader, but only through investments, speculation in property and other essentially parasitic schemes, all sanitized by the euphemisms of the fi-nancial industry. For those whose only source of income is the "sweat of their brow," their chances of getting ahead are gen-erally low. And while the ordinary person may ride on the coattails of the "capital gains" and also do well for a while, perhaps by investing in property, they are but feeding on the drippings.

A convergence of trends

The advent of this distortion in the relationship between honest work and the accumulation of wealth is also partly a result of other destabilizing social and economic trends, which are further challenging the economic model that is based on ever-expanding, unrepayable debt.

One of them is globalization. While it is a force that drives economic growth in developing countries around the world, it has resulted in fewer and lower-paying jobs for ordinary wage-earners in developed countries, since most manufacturing and many service jobs have moved to developing nations because of their much lower labor and regulatory costs.

At the same time, the inexorable march of new technology has made many jobs redundant, and will continue to do so at an increasing pace.

Add to this the demographic shift to an aging population in many developed and developing nations, with notable exceptions among the developing ones, such as Iran and Brazil, with an ever-greater proportion of retirees in which there are ever-fewer people available to work to service the debts. In a system dependent on ever-increasing levels of debt, this is very problematic.

Education

The hollowing-out of productive occupations in Western societies, along with the devaluation of honorable work, has diminished the value of another pillar of modern society, education. As it becomes clear that it is no longer the reliable pathway to middle-class security and respectability that it once might have been, its romanticized position as a magic elixir against inequality is being challenged. Even when a good job can be secured upon graduation, graduates are faced with the prospect of repaying onerous student loan debt, servicing mortgages on exorbitantly expensive houses, and paying taxes to keep mountains of government debt from collapsing.

All of this has been brought about by a shift in the economic model, whereby the financial world has become outsized in proportion to the productive world. Now the people employed to do real work are, in essence, indebted serfs, paying a tithe to those few who are the beneficiaries of the financial industry.

The ethos of entitlement

The prospects of the general population are also diminished by a pervasive culture of entitlement, which spans the economic spectrum, encompassing both the rich and the poor. It is easy to blame the poor, some of whom appear to believe that the government owes them a living, but this criticism is equally applicable to the rich, who want the government to extend to them protection and special privileges at the expense of everyone else. The popular refrain of "Why doesn't the government do something about it?" is symptomatic of this dysfunction: government agencies are expected to be all things to all people, while personal responsibility has been demoted from a social requirement to an optional virtue. Pushing back, government agencies have also sought to saddle people with responsibility, often in inappropriate contexts, creating an uneasy dissonance where responsibility without control produces stress.

Our political systems offer little that can inspire hope or effect positive change. Vaguely different parties roll out predictable party lines about change and choice, but deliver little that is any different. A pretense of political choice is maintained by robust debate about systemically insignificant points, and more than likely you would want to vote for the least worst of the two usual choices, but that is about it. Indeed, the question could be posed: Is there anything worth voting for at all? Nothing ever really changes when one party replaces another in the antiquated and dysfunctional electoral systems of quasi-representation that have been foisted on us. Our political leaders may tinker with the system, but their efforts generally amount to little more than bluster and self-interested pomposity.

Interestingly, growing public disillusionment with the political process is splitting the electorate into extremes of left and right. Fed up with the largely facile nature of politics and seeing through the emptiness of the words being thrown around, voters are developing a taste for something that is more authentic. But it would seem that it will take more than radical opinions for there to be effective change, and there is quite a large gap to be bridged between the proponents of a swing to the left and a swing to the right.

Is it any different in the developing world?

Young people in developing countries are faced with a different set of circumstances. There, the vital energy of unbridled capitalism (fueled by a competitive advantage over their Western counterparts), combined with technology, abundant cheap labor and access to resources, have propelled many to a better standard of living and a buoyant sense of self-confidence. This has emboldened the aspirations of the populations of countries such as India, China, Russia and Brazil, and many in these nations have been honeymooning in a cocoon of consumerist euphoria.

But despite the indisputable improvements in their material state, there is a lingering doubt as to whether the present course of the developing world holds much hope for their populations. The young masses of these countries now share the limitations of the lifestyles experienced by their Western peers, finding themselves paying high rents and large mortgages for small, overpriced apartments, working vaguely fulfilling jobs that lack meaningful human contact, and finding solace in material trinkets and the prospect of the occasional holiday. Without the social safety nets afforded by the liberal West, they are also surrounded by the poverty of those who haven't been swept up in the leap of consumerist progress, and this also creates a problem: it is difficult to enjoy one's expensive branded coffee when there is stark suffering staring you in the face from across the street.

In our interconnected world, the economic destiny of these nations is also imperiled by the sickly state of Western economies. The entire world economy operates on fiat currencies which have no inherent value, and, given the way these are being treated by the central bankers of the world, they are only one really bad trading week away from being rendered worthless. Nobody can predict with confidence when this day will come; nor can anyone argue persuasively that it won't come.

A breakdown in the narrative

The integrity of the narrative we have been conditioned to accept as the truth—one of trust in education, hard work, saving one's money, and of what passes for democracy, is being eroded. There are powerful forces at work, desperately holding together the system that sustains the positions of the technocrats, the oligarchs and the arms dealers—those who benefit from it—while keeping the rest of us working as obedient debt-servicing serfs. But the effects of their machinations are fading. People everywhere are becoming unsettled by the status quo, and while they might not understand the details or know what to do about it, they are getting the feeling that something really isn't right.

Our environment

Here there are numerous problems: soil degradation, water resource depletion, climate change, loss of biodiversity, ocean acidification, problems with the containment of nuclear waste and many other issues. If the current economic system is allowed to carry on its current trajectory, they will increasingly impinge upon the lives of ordinary people in a significant, life-threatening way. While time horizons are difficult to predict with any degree of certainty, there is complete agreement about the mathematical realities of trends that are on a collision course with finite limits—ones that no defender of our current model of ever-faster squandering of environmental capital can logically dispute.

Science is unequivocal that we cannot have a system dependent on infinite growth on a planet with finite resources, and the thought that we should keep it going for as long as possible is fundamentally faulty. Already gone are plentiful fish stocks, abundant free-flowing crude oil, fresh uncultivated arable land and an unpolluted atmosphere. All of these things are now in the past as far as humanity's time on Earth is concerned. We are destined to live out the rest of our time as a species on a significantly different planet from the one on which we evolved and multiplied.

Like the awakening that is happening in relation to our economic realities, there is also a crystallization of understanding among all people of the world, west, east, north, and south, about the callous way in which our environment is becoming ever more degraded for the sake of industrial progress. Numerous people express the ardent desire to do more to live in harmony with the Earth's natural systems, yet all but a few lack the means or the knowledge to truly do this. For as long as we carry on along our current economic path, such positive change remains impossible.

Our moral position

In assessing our moral position, Mahatma Gandhi presented a contemporary variant on the seven deadly sins of Christian ethics, which have been more kindly described as the Seven Blunders of the World:

Wealth without Work.
Pleasure without Conscience.
Science without Humanity.
Knowledge without Character.

Politics without Principle.
Commerce without Morality.
Worship without Sacrifice.

A look at these seven measures shows that there is much
blundering in the world at present.

Wealth without work might
as well be the motto of the financial industry that dominates the
global economy, in which traders

Mahatma Gandhi

make money out of skimming off the income of productive
workers while doing no real productive work themselves. For
example, they can pick up ten cents on the dollar by trading
corn futures, driving up the price of corn in times of drought,
and gouging all the people who have to eat. Whatever their
justifications may be, this doesn't contribute much in the way
of goodness to the world.

An evening spent watching television will produce enough
evidence to show that the phrase **pleasure without conscience** does capture something of the zeitgeist of our times.
The mix of celebrity news, oriented around excess and the
worship of indulgence, reality television in which producers
cultivate narratives based around people being selfish toward
each other, and soap operas where the superficial emotions
such as self-pity, resentment and jealousy are presented as the
norm, presents a bleak picture of the general human condition. Add to this the pervasive licentiousness evident everywhere and the pernicious effect of advertising, which is almost

all based on idiocentric body satisfaction, and it becomes clear that there is a torrent of suggestion being constantly directed at the general population which acts to separate its members from their conscience.

The perversity of **science without humanity** is clear in a world where there is an ongoing wave of technological progress, but where the fruits of these advances are so unevenly divided and so often used against each other in maleficent ways. One example of this lack of humanity is in modern food production, which is so efficient that we could easily provide enough to feed everyone, yet there is still widespread hunger. The World Food Program statistics state that in 2015 there will be an estimated 3.1 million hunger-related deaths in children under five. Another example: science has facilitated the creation of new modes of warfare with an increasingly dangerous potential. Men and women sitting in air-conditioned offices in Nevada spend their days piloting drone aircraft, with which they blow up people, cars and buildings in foreign countries on the other side of the planet, as if playing a video game, while ostensibly living otherwise normal lives. The decontextualization of the relationship between the killers and the killed, and the huge inaccuracies inherent in this system, produce an inhuman and arbitrary killing machine. (Leaked US military information on the success of a five-month period of drone strikes in Afghanistan revealed that nine out of ten times they resulted in the deaths of unintended targets.) Not only is this unfair to the people accidentally killed and maimed by these remotely deployed bombs, it is also psychologically destructive to the military personnel being asked to deploy them, and an agent of cultural brutalization on both sides.

Nicholas Butler described an expert as "one who knows more and more about less and less." To which the byline: "to the point where they know everything about nothing" can be added. Oscar Wilde wrote that "Nowadays people know the price of everything, and the value of nothing." Both quotes illustrating the extent toward which knowledge and understanding can diverge. In this "information age" where higher education and specialization have spawned monolithic institutions of bureaucracy and entrenched modes of arbitrary thinking, it can be seen that **knowledge without character** is an inherent danger. Ivory tower authority, and unscrutinized opinion peddled as fact in the media have created a situation where simplistic righteousness prevails more often than not, devoid of the nuance and subtlety inherent in character.

With the rise of fundamentalist extremism we see the most outrageous examples of **politics without principle**, and the crimes that are being perpetrated in the name of peace and security can scarcely be believed. Little more needs to be said about this!

Likewise, **commerce without morality** is something we have all experienced, and it is so prevalent that it requires no further description.

Worship without sacrifice is descriptive of our current culture of instant gratification, and the example of Gandhi, who endured great personal hardships for the sake of his beliefs, is at odds with the easy-speak produced by the speech writers and focus groups who concoct the hollow words of most of our modern moral leaders.

Nature abhors a vacuum

Despite the situation just described, there is not much of an opposing force against the system that perpetuates this set of circumstances. Rather, there is a vacuum: no note to sound against the status quo, and a profound lack of positive aspiration. The deep-rooted and pervasive institutions that sustain and protect this self-destructive mode of existence function virtually unopposed.

Gazing into this void, we can take solace in the observation attributed to the ancient Greek philosopher Aristotle: Nature abhors a vacuum. An empty space will not remain empty for long, for the dynamism and creativity of nature will fill it quickly. A plowed field will sprout weeds, wind disturbs still air and the mind refuses to sit vacant. While we may lament the vacuum inside the hearts and minds of so many people in the world at present, it is the way of nature that they will be filled.

Aristotle

In this void, what is missing is a story of hope—one that is authentic, intelligent and provides something different and tangible for people to believe in.

Our systems of government, commerce and social organization are failing us, and our current experiment in civilization has fallen out of line with natural laws in so many ways that at some point in the future a crisis seems all but inevitable. In spite of this, this is a time of great potential, when small beginnings can lead to dramatic results. The vacuum that is being created as the current system decays creates a space for something new.

It is likely that there will be pain ahead, but also the hope that in the process of breaking the shackles of our current system we may learn to live by a different code. In taking stock, there is also much that is positive that should be acknowledged, and in looking to the future we can also find solace in that which is good in the human spirit.

Fumbling for answers

Throughout history, civilizations, cultures, nations and economies have ebbed and flowed, the mighty have risen and fallen, and utopia has been repeatedly demonstrated to be an illusion. The history of man is littered with the follies of idealists, half-baked philosophies and vaguely hopeful movements. In assessing solutions to the problems of the present day, there are many pitfalls. It could be said that none of us are sufficiently detached and objective to gauge the situation with complete rationality.

On this, Vivekananda, a wise Indian sage, and a prominent founding father of modern India, cautioned that "This world is like a dog's curly tail. People have been striving to straighten it out for hundreds of years; but when they let it go, it has curled up again." Nevertheless, it is necessary that we try to understand the world around us, for there are serious questions to be pondered:

What sense is to be made of our supposed environmental and economic problems?

What can be done to alleviate the suffering of our fellow brothers and sisters?

Vivekananda

What is our strategy for moving forward into the future in a more sustainable way?

These are perennial questions, but now, more so than ever, the answers that have served us well in the past need to be remembered for the present day. Many of the failings of our current system of organization are clear, but amongst the abundance of commentaries on what the problems are, there is no alternative philosophy that inspires conviction.

Winston Churchill

Winston Churchill, in his oft-repeated quote that "democracy is the worst form of Government except all those other forms that have been tried" could have said the same of our current system of resource utilization. For it seems that free-market capitalism is the worst economic system ever—except for

33

all the others that have been tried: Communism, Fascism and the idealism of the sixties have all failed, and a return to Feudalism or the simple life of pre-modern indigenous cultures is something that few of us would look forward to. It is as though our current model of Liberal Democratic Capitalism has won the crown in a beauty pageant of many contenders, all of them horribly ugly. The outcomes that it delivers are the least bad, and while for a select few the outcomes are very good, overall it is a system that is obviously leading us to a dead end.

Root cause analysis

Albert Einstein, who was a philosopher as well as a scientist, placed great emphasis on the need to ponder when approaching problem solving. He went to great lengths to refine the questions that he asked, for he understood that if he could ask the right questions, and hold them central to his thinking, then the answers would present themselves accordingly. But most attempts at analyzing our degradation of the environment and the shortcomings of our

Albert Einstein

system of economics fail, because they fail to ask the appropriate questions—ones that would allow them to arrive at the root cause of what is wrong.

2. An Alternative Frame of Reference

First principles

Those who have been trained as engineers or scientists are predisposed to investigate problems starting from first principles: to establish what is known at the most basic level—just the facts, so to speak—and then build a conclusion based on logic. When we attempt to analyze our current system using such a method, we must first backtrack quite far, dispensing with received certainties imparted to us through various official channels which may or may not have a basis in fact. Instead, we must seek to see things from a fresh perspective, outside of the prism of ordinary thinking. And to do this systematically, we first need to establish an alternative frame of reference.

Newton's third law

The laws of physics may seem an unlikely place to start when approaching an analysis of our system of economics, but Newton's third law describes a dynamic that is universal in all systems, not just mechanical:

**For every action, there is an equal
and opposite reaction.**

This law characterizes a system in which there are three forces at work: the action, the reaction, and the organizing principle according to which this dynamic is resolved, which is the conserva-

Newton's Third Law

tion of energy. This triadic interplay exists in all dynamic systems, and while in some systems it may seem chaotic, there will always be an organizing principle that reconciles the conflict between an initial impulse and its eventual negation. Its application is straightforward in the analysis of physical systems, where the organizing principles are the laws of physics, but, interestingly, it is also applicable to psychology and group dynamics, where the organizing principle may be some framework of identity, social convention or externally applied set of rules.

Let us call this organizing principle the "reconciling force."

The Tao and physics

The Tao

The Taoist symbol of yin and yang also provides a useful context. While the introduction of a symbol from the realm of metaphysics may seem like an unusual departure in a discussion of sustainability and economics, this symbol is useful for conveying knowledge at the level of fundamentals and helpful in our aim to understand the significance of the incentive structure behind our current system.

In the symbol of the Tao, the two fields—one black, the other white—represent the pair of opposites, and ordinarily this is about as much as people would see: two opposing forces working against each other, yin and yang, action and reaction, masculine and feminine. Less obvious, but perfectly intuitive once you put your mind to it, and essential to the emergent significance of the symbol, is that it also represents a third force: the harmony that is manifested in the entire symbol, where yin and yang are held in balance, in equal proportions, which represents the organizing principle, or the reconciling force. In Taoist philosophy, without black there could be no white, and for both to exist they must be held in eternal balance by the action of the unknowable Tao.

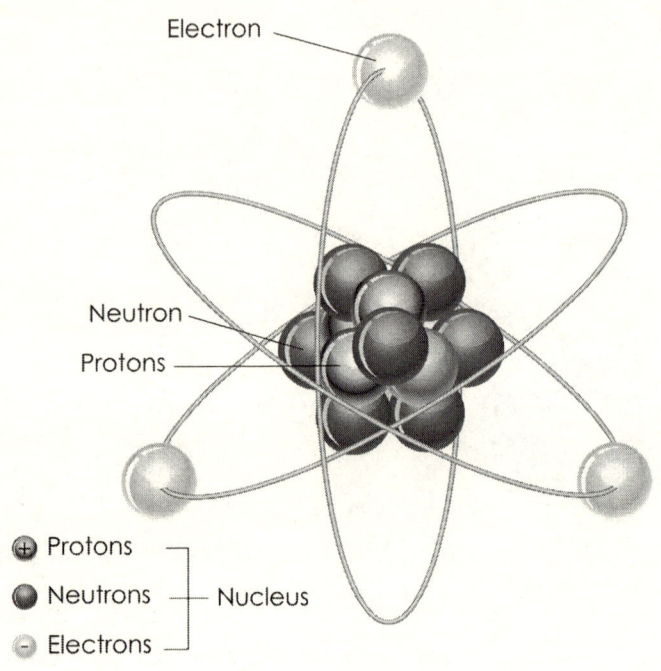

Electron

Neutron

Protons

⊕ Protons ⌉
● Neutrons ├ Nucleus
⊖ Electrons ⌋

Structure of the Atom

The dynamic of action, reaction and reconciliation is also evident in the structure of an atom, where there are also three elements present: the positively-charged protons and the negatively-charged electrons interact to form stable elements, facilitated by the presence of neutrally-charged neutrons. In this example, the neutrons are the reconciling force, and from this simple triadic template comes all matter in the universe.

An example from our everyday lives

Extending this triadic dynamic to human interaction, we can observe that in any situation where there is a process of initiation and negation, the same type of system is at work. Any effort to make a change in any direction always meets with a response in the form of opposition. This conflict is resolved according to the predominant organizing principle in effect at the time. Here again there are three forces at work: action, reaction and reconciliation.

One example of such a system that most of us can relate to in a human context is marriage: when two people make a commitment to share their lives together, there is an organizing principle that holds them together, whether they are aware of this or not. It is the glue that sustains the relationship, and the reference point from which a couple can resolve its differences. Be it a complex web of mutual dependence, a sense of responsibility before children and other family members or, in the worst case, a vain sense of social propriety, it is the reconciling force of their relationship.

Often the force that initially catalyzes a relationship is sexual attraction, which is a powerful and ubiquitous force of nature. But usually it is not an enduring force due to the propensity for sexual attraction to become less of a motivator when faced with more everyday stressors, like the need to keep the kitchen sink clear of dirty dishes and maintaining general household order.

Another common reconciling force in a marriage (often taking over gradually as sexual attraction fades) is the welfare of the children, where the parents meet each other halfway to reconcile their conflicting individual needs for the benefit of the whole family. The welfare of the children then becomes the predominant organizing principle.

And even in a dysfunctional marriage—for example, where the motivating force of the welfare of the children has lost its intensity—the reconciling force may be the fear of separation. Each person is afraid of becoming poorer should they part ways, or of the separation being too shameful or too difficult. In this case, the organizing principle isn't anything particularly positive, but it does keep the two together. On the other hand, in a healthy marriage there is usually some positive ideal or shared system of belief that is the reconciling force, such as an abiding friendship underpinned by acceptance, loyalty and love.

Triads within triads

If we look closely at the two elements that are in opposition within a triad, we can often discern that they too contain opposing elements moderated by some organizing principle: there are triads within triads, all the way down.

Consider any job. Here, there is a triad that exists between the employer and the employee, moderated by the employment contract. At times a worker and a boss may disagree, and when they do their dispute can be resolved by recourse to the employment contract, which is the reconciling force. But at a more basic level there is an internal battle that goes on inside the mind of the worker. The worker chose to accept the job—we may call that the initiating force. Conflicting with it is the fact that, more likely than not, the employee doesn't like the job, and, more specifically, may not want to perform certain duties, finding them tedious or unpleasant. This conflict is usually reconciled by the employee's need for money, which is the organizing principle.

Seeing the world from the perspective of Newton's third law

Thus we see that the dynamic described by Newton's Third Law provides a method for understanding a great many things. It can even be seen as universally applicable.[6]

In light of Einstein's maxim—that one must first think hard about which questions to ask when trying to solve a problem—it would seem important that we try and understand the workings of this dynamic in our society at present. The fundamental questions are these:

1. What is the major reconciling force that governs our system of politics and economics today?

2. What are the effects of this reconciling force?

3. If there were to be a new reconciling force, what would it be?

And it is here that I wish to make a bold statement: It would take little more than effectively answering these three questions for our lives to change for the better, for that which follows from such a basic understanding becomes inevitable. By analyzing our world on the basis of first principles, we become, to quote Luke 6:48, "like a man which built an house, and digged deep, and laid the foundation on a rock: and when the flood arose, the stream beat vehemently upon that house, and could not shake it: for it was founded upon a rock."

---

6 For further discussion on the topic, the discipline of Systematics is an interesting reference point.

3. Capitalism

The profit motive

Let us explicitly address the three questions posed at the end of the last chapter.

The dominant reconciling force in all of our worldly affairs at present is the profit motive, and the effects of that cannot be overstated. It is the organizing principle that we operate by above all others.

For while there are many other values that may be considered important in our society—social justice, environmental protection, community engagement—no enterprise can survive without surplus assets generated by profit. And without profitable businesses a country or a region will not have the tax revenues to fund its activities, and it too will fail. Profit is therefore imperative, and in the administration of the affairs of state and business all other aims are secondary.

Translated into every-day life, there is a simple creed from *David Copperfield* by Charles Dickens: "Annual income twenty pounds, annual expenditure nineteen [pounds] nineteen [shillings] and six [pence], result happiness. Annual income twenty pounds, annual expenditure twenty pounds ought and six, result misery." It expresses the relationship that is

Charles Dickens

fundamental to the capitalist system and goes some way to explaining how the reconciling force of the profit motive shapes much of the world as we know it. It is a precondition of success in our modern society that we must remain financially solvent, and in order to do this profit is paramount.

Before we can further explain the technical details of how the profit motive manifests itself as a reconciling force, we first need to identify two other forces: the creative force of entrepreneurship and the constraining force of limited resources. Not all entrepreneurs can succeed in their ventures, because only the most profitable can survive.

The "invisible hand" of the market that Adam Smith spoke of in *The Wealth of Nations* is a metaphor he employed to describe how individuals acting in their own economic self-interest serve to benefit society directly. The inference he made is

Adam Smith

that the actions of individuals seeking to make a profit through their entrepreneurial efforts in the marketplace will serve society by helping to establish an equilibrium between the supply and demand of goods. The market thus serves to allocate resources to the most profitable enterprises, ignoring the rest, and, in doing so, those products and services that society wants are provided at a cost that it is prepared to pay.

The limits on social responsibility and ethical standards

The renowned 20th-century economist Milton Friedman also understood something of the objective rationality of the profit motive, and one of his more controversial theories stated that, provided it does not break the law, under no circumstances should a business aim to do anything other than make a profit. He believed that social responsibility was a fundamentally subversive doctrine, and was scathing of those who claimed that businesses should concern themselves with promoting desirable social ends. In Friedman's view, it would be tantamount to treason if a business executive were to consider taking on responsibility for "providing employment, eliminating discrimination, avoiding pollution and whatever else may be the catchwords of the contemporary crop of reformers."[7] While it may be controversial and somewhat ruthless, the validity of his theory is apparent: shareholders have the right to sue the directors of a public company if they believe the directors are not acting in their interests to maximize profits.

In practice, there are many shades of gray

Milton Friedman

associated with the implementation of this statute, and businesses adopt various policies of social responsibility to further their interests, their motives ranging from altruistic at the positive end of the scale to calculated and self-serving at the other. Somewhere in the middle of this range is the theory of green economics, which holds that consumers will pay extra for environmentally friendly products, thus aligning the social good of environmental protection with the business aim of profit. Accordingly, a chicken farmer is able to sell free-range eggs for a higher price to those who oppose the cruel practice of keeping hens in cages.

But when businesses face an ethical choice that does not result in increased profitability, the choice of business execu-

---

7 New York Times Magazine, September 13, 1970

tives ultimately comes down to whether to remain in business or not. Regardless of the level of social or environmental aspirations of a private enterprise, the underlying reconciling factor must always be profit, because without profit the enterprise will cease to exist, along with its superior moral and ethical stance.

And so there are many questionable situations that arise in our society that are accepted as normal, because companies must compromise their ethical standards in their quest for profits. To sell their product, cereal companies put so much sugar in children's breakfasts that it is damaging to their health. Moneylenders make people slaves to debt by giving loans to those who are in no position to repay them. Casinos make money from gambling addicts, and furniture companies make furniture from old-growth rainforests. Supermarkets sell tuna caught from stocks that are overfished and approaching extinction. Food companies douse the soil with pesticides, killing the life of the land. Alcohol and tobacco companies market to the addicted and the vulnerable. Employers put thousands of people out of work at short notice to beat analysts' expectations. Mining companies build mountains of toxic tailings that leach into the groundwater. Media companies exploit the suffering of grieving people to sell newspapers and magazines. Arms manufacturers sell advanced weapons systems to murderous regimes. Power companies build nuclear power plants on earthquake fault lines. The litany of examples of compromised ethics goes on and on, and there are many thousands of books and films that bear witness to them and the suffering that they cause.

Even a seemingly exemplary company such as Google, which even has a slogan of "Don't be evil" and a famous reputation for taking good care of its employees, has been found to be deeply compromised. It has been variously accused of facilitating a massive and illegal spying campaign by a US government agency, engaging in anticompetitive behaviors which inhibit the emergence of potential competitors and seeking to protect itself using deceitful public relations campaigns. This is not to say that Google is an altogether evil company, because it is involved in many interesting ventures with considerable potential for public good, but the environment in which it operates makes it impossible for it live up to the exalted standard to which its slogan aspires.

The profit motive is inherently negative

A basic effect of the profit motive on society is that it promotes a gross form of selfishness. The imperative of the marketplace to make a profit means that there is little room for sentiment, for the niceties of human dignity or compassion, because if you take your eye off the bottom line someone will take over your market share and muscle you out of business. There are a few moderating influences: the influence of the self-aware, ethically-attuned consumers (who swiftly turn into price-sensitive consumers as soon as ethics impinges on their spending power); attempts at regulation through law (which is a clumsy instrument); and the innate goodness of people that shines through in some situations. But in the game of capitalism the most selfish participants generally come out to be the winners.

Aldous Huxley

The profit motive also promotes greed in its most potent form by encouraging hoarding: the successful competitors strive to accumulate a larger surplus than their rivals, because the bigger their pile, the more secure their position. This creates a class of wealthy people who, with an overabundance of resources at their disposal, are able to enjoy material pleasures to an excess, while others are forced to live without even the basic necessities. That class of wealthy people is also able to indulge in the more subtle psychological pleasure of exhibiting their influence and self-importance, which accrues to them through their control of resources. In turn, this creates divisions in society and establishes hereditary privileged groups, which further amplify these patterns of greed over time.

In any situation where there is greed, at the opposite swing of the pendulum there awaits its faithful companion—fear. For those who have wealth, there is the eternal fear of losing it, and for those who have never had wealth in the first place there is the fear of not being able to survive and make their way in a world dominated by greed and selfishness. While we teach our children not to be selfish, greedy or afraid, we do all we can to perpetuate

Ayn Rand

a system that has these three negativities at its very core. How can we expect our children not to see us as hypocrites?

Aldous Huxley suggested that "Our present economic, social and international arrangements are based, in large measure, upon organized lovelessness," and, on the evidence, it appears that he was right. Our current system, governed by the reconciling force of profit motive, is dominated by greed and fear—certainly not love! This is a fact that even the most fervent supporters of the capitalist system cannot hope to refute, and while some, such as the libertarian devotees of Ayn Rand, somehow find it possible to rejoice in it, it stands to reason that if we continue on this path of embracing profoundly negative values, it will surely lead us to our destruction.

Law as a counterpart to the profit motive

In a system governed by the profit motive, where the marketplace pits rivals against each other in fierce competition, the law acts to provide a moderating context. In an environment where there is much at stake,

Scales of Justice, London Criminal Court

and the spoils of victory great, it is necessary that there be rules in place to maintain some basic standards, and to prevent capitalism from degenerating into gangsterism, or worse.

For example, slavery used to be legal in many parts of the world, but is now banned by a binding international convention (at least in its most overt and blatant forms). At the opposite end of the spectrum, in England it was once a common practice for bakers to add such things as ground bones, clay and chalk to bread to keep costs down and increase profits, but now this is also illegal.

For a business, compliance with the laws is usually seen as a cost, especially when it comes to environmental regulations and labor laws. And since minimizing costs to maximize profits is part of Friedman's ideological imperative, businesses tend to gravitate to locations where the laws are the least restrictive. As long as property and contract law are respected, fewer laws generally mean greater profits.

Financial services companies have been very active in extorting governments to enact lax laws that support their doubtful activities. They threaten to move their operations offshore to jurisdictions with less regulation unless they get their way, and thus deny their resident economies of high-paying jobs and tax revenues. With very few exceptions, governments have acceded to their demands. Another form of support they have been able to extort is tax money: whenever their "too big to fail" backsides need to be bailed out as a consequence of their reckless, unregulated risk-taking, it is the taxpayers who have been forced to pick up the bill, suffering through austerity and higher taxes. And the latest form of banker welfare, first tested on Cyprus in 2013, is the so-called "bail-in," in which bank deposits are looted to refloat insolvent banks. A year later, at the G-20 meeting in Brisbane, this strategy was given overall approval, changing the rules of banking so that bank deposits can now be confiscated at will.

A similar trend has been apparent in global manufacturing. Over the past three decades global manufacturing has gravitated toward countries such as China, which have very lax environmental laws, and little in the way of enforcement of the few environmental laws they do have. There are huge cost savings to be had when a manufacturer need not be concerned about the impact of its waste, if it is not necessary to implement safety protocols to prevent the accidental discharge of pollutants, and if it cannot be held liable for the damage its operations cause to public health.

Pity the poor fish in the rivers, though.

The costs of employment are also much greater in most developed countries, where regulations require that workers be kept safe, paid for their holidays, provided with employment contracts, not be forcibly confined or physically

Fish vs. pollution

abused, and generally treated with a modicum of dignity. Therefore, companies in search of higher profits through lower costs will also tend to utilize labor in less-regulated countries, where workers have many fewer rights, bypassing the costly burden of providing decent work for decent wages.

Thus we can see that the usefulness of the law as a moderating context for capitalism in the world of international business is somewhat limited.

The law is a blunt instrument

The law is based upon the interpretation of rules that are written so as to be as general as possible, but they are subsequently applied in very specific circumstances. This conceptual flaw means that laws inherently lack sensitivity and contextual nuance, and the inevitable shades of grey present in any real-world situation have to be resolved by lawyers who argue endlessly about the meanings of words, taking a lot of time and costing extravagant amounts of money. In the process, they tend to divide people into winners and losers, giving rise to feelings of loss, aggravation and resentment.

The law is based on the precise interpretation of words, making it vulnerable to exploitation by clever people who find loopholes that go against the intent of the law. This creates a culture of insincerity, in which various parties adopt positions of righteousness that are not backed up by any sense of morality, and use tortuous language to disguise their pursuit of self-interest.

The very process by which laws are formulated requires them to be complex, since the process of developing them requires many different situations to be considered, and many different contexts to be accommodated. But no matter how intricate and nuanced a piece of legislation, most situations in which it applies do not allow for intricacy or nuance. They usually involve people or companies with limited amounts of experience, competence and resources. Thus, no matter how perfect a law is in its conception, it inevitably becomes a blunt instrument in its application.

The law upholds privilege

One further significant shortcoming of the law is that it is biased in favor of those with money. The cost of engaging lawyers to resolve a dispute in the courts is significant, and those with the biggest budgets—insurance companies and other large corporations—have a far greater ability to prevail in litigation than ordinary citizens. There is often a total mismatch between parties that are in disagreement. A lawsuit is a small risk for corporations, with their armies of lawyers and with millions or billions of dollars in their war chests. To battle them, private citizens may have to stake their life's savings and commit a significant portion of their lives.

Moreover, the law provides numerous advantages to wealthy and powerful people looking to protect their interests. It is a powerful enabling medium for numerous strategies that prevail through obfuscation, deceitfulness and insincerity in

Protesting the death of Eric Garner, killed by police in New York, 2014

the pursuit of naked self-interest. These include the use of complicated small print to shirk moral responsibility, the structuring of one's affairs in order to avoid taxation, the evasion of personal responsibility by establishing limited liability legal vehicles and, as just mentioned, by bullying those who are poorer and thus weaker with the threat of litigation.

Lastly, the law allows for systemic, legalized corruption. Those with money and connections can usually find a way to exert undue influence on lawmakers—through political donations, lobbying and more corrupt means—to have laws enacted that favor their private interests at the expense of the public. The outcome of this situation in the United States is particularly glaring. Petty criminals, even very young ones, are imprisoned or killed for such offenses as stealing a sandwich or selling loose cigarettes. At the same time, bankers who fraudulently manipulate markets to make billions of dollars in profits and tens of millions in bonuses for themselves escape either without any penalties at all, or by paying a fine—because they have prevailed upon the courts to treat them as, of all things, juvenile delinquents.[8]

The law stifles personal responsibility

Finally, and paradoxically, the law also tends to stifle personal responsibility and initiative by imposing a heavy burden of compliance. Taking the United Kingdom as an example, there are over 21,000 pieces of regulation covering all manner of situations. Instead of nurturing self-reliance and furthering the

---

8 In the scandals exposed in the aftermath of the Global Financial Crisis in 2007 the US Justice Department routinely negotiated with lawyers to impose deferred prosecution agreements (DPAs) on financial industry executives actually caught ripping off the rest of society. DPAs were established as a mechanism for giving young first time offenders committing misdemeanor crimes a second chance. Conveniently, these agreements also mean that the perpetrators need not bear the indignity of standing trial, or suffer the inconvenience of a criminal conviction, which might otherwise have crimped their style when vacationing abroad, or inhibited their future job prospects.

development of good judgment, many of these regulations seek to protect people from themselves. Children—even teenagers—cannot play unattended. Blind obedience to rules and mechanically generating health and safety compliance paperwork have become more important than safety itself. For example, a school in Bristol in the United Kingdom recently banned a blind 7-year-old girl from using her cane because it constituted a trip hazard. Examples of this absurd lack of common sense abound in the culture of zealous compliance that colors most of the Western world. All of this leads to an increasingly enfeebled population, fit only for life in a climate-controlled padded cell under the watchful eye of certified, credentialed minders. The root cause of this insanity is reliance on the law as a reconciling force, while what is really needed is discretion and intelligence.

Having such an overbearing level of regulatory demands makes people afraid to do things, and as a consequence they play it safe and become risk-averse. It would be much better for people to be able to give things a go without fear of being tripped up by the details of some unfathomable regulation they did not know existed.

The law is a poor foil for the ills of the profit motive

Regulation is often put forward as a way of compensating for the numerous ills created by the profit motive. But this amounts to an attempt to use two wrongs to make a right, because, just like the profit motive itself, the law is also rooted in negativity. It is a way of setting parties apart in conflict. As noted above, it promotes insincerity, disguises the pursuit of naked self-interest, amplifies the effects of privilege, and is slow, cumbersome, expensive, imprecise and unpredictable in its application, and vulnerable to exploitation and misappropriation by the least scrupulous.

That is not to say that lawlessness should be encouraged or promoted. But at the granular level where the socials ills borne of the profit motive have to be opposed, the usefulness of the law is very limited, and recourse to it is fraught with un-intended consequences.

Conclusions

In concluding this negative assessment of the capitalist system, it cannot go unsaid that the profit motive has generated many positive outcomes. Coupled with an abundance of conve-nient, energy-rich crude oil and with dramatic advances in science and technology, it has undoubtedly enabled much progress for humankind—though much of it may prove to be transitory, undone by resource depletion and environmental devastation.

Because the profit motive provides for the concentration of capital, innovators and risk-takers have been able to secure funding for advances in industry and technology which have brought us to the zenith of the information age. We now have the wondrous capacity of the internet, which gives us nearly instantaneous access to almost any piece of information lo-cated anywhere in the world from wherever we happen to be. It has also facilitated the development of pharmaceuticals that have revolutionized healthcare, and, through the agents of mass production and specialization, has dramatically im-proved food production, construction and education, although quality may have been sacrificed for the sake of quantity in the pursuit of such improvements, and although the methods used are highly unsustainable.

However, planted into the heart of the capitalist system are the seeds of its own destruction. The profit motive is a negative force, restraining us from the pursuit of the public good by prioritizing profits above all else. Law, as a moderating influence on the profit motive, is also, in practice, a negative force, restraining freedom of action and repressing individual judgment and responsibility. Negativity begets negativity, and, gradually but inexorably, the numerous ways in which capitalism fouls its own nest reinforce each other and, in the end, threaten to undo all of its temporary victories.

The social fabric that holds together the institutions of capitalism is already threadbare. It is a system with a limited future. I believe that it has largely run its course, and that we are ready for the next stage in our evolution. Selfishness, fear and greed are base emotions, and it is our challenge to rise above our worst nature and to establish a common, positive reconciling force for humankind that can bring about a more enlightened state of existence.

4. Communism

Whenever someone attempts a critique of capitalism, communism suddenly springs forth, like the bogeyman, rearing its ugly head from a territory where only fools would dare to tread. This generally ends the discussion—quite understandably, given how little praise most people can come up with for the various experiments that have branded themselves as communist. Their lasting impressions are from the television images of the Soviet era: bread lines, the threat of nuclear war, military parades, Ladas, lots of vodka and endless, featureless rows of gray concrete apartment buildings. This is not a picture of prosperity. At odds with this view are reminiscences of a big chunk of the population of the former USSR, even many of those born after 1991—the year it was dissolved—who continue to wax nostalgic about the good old Soviet days.

When summarizing history, there is a tendency to recount the stories of those who have experienced extremes. In the case of the Soviets they are about hard labor in Siberia, the brutality of the Afghan war and other topics out of the ordinary. But for the majority life was more mundane and settled, and their stories are not part of the legacy of the Soviet era that is well known in the West. For the ordinary person there was much that was missed when the Soviet Union collapsed, as is described by Ukrainian writer Andrei Kurkov:

"That society was founded on friendship. You could knock at your neighbor's door and if you needed money, they would lend it to you. All that solidarity collapsed with the break-up of the Soviet Union. People born just before that, now in their 20s, adapt very quickly. For my generation, solitude is the scourge of life today. I've lost many friends. Many have committed suicide; others have emigrated."

Andrei Kurkov

But it is rather telling that even those who bemoan the Soviet collapse are still unlikely to vote communist. They appear to be fine with capitalism.

China—the sole remaining significant communist-run country in the world—is sometimes said to be, in fact, more capitalist than all the capitalist nations, and quite successful at it too, having grown to be the world's largest economy. In reality, China's success came in large part from its ability to cleverly combine elements of free-market capitalism, state capitalism, and socialism. Despite this seeming rejection of communism, it was not rejected outright, and there are aspects of China's socialist fabric that have enabled it to achieve the rapid growth and success witnessed in the last two decades.

The remaining communist-run nation-states—North Korea, Cuba and Laos—are not helpful in the cause of promoting communism either, North Korea and Cuba because the continuous bad press they receive precludes any possibility of an objective assessment, and Laos because it receives no press at all. Repressive dictatorships do deserve bad press, but that is not to say that there aren't any elements in the ordinary experience of communist living in these countries that we might appreciate.

And so let's ignore the nonissue of how communism and capitalism might stack up against each other—because they don't. They are certainly not in any sort of competition at the moment. But communism has been shown to work, after a fashion, in various countries and for extended periods of time. At one point it worked well enough to defeat Hitler, to make American schoolchildren climb under their school desks in anticipation of nuclear annihilation, to provide large-scale development assistance to much of the developing world and to stymie the US military by trapping it in a series of unsuccessful proxy wars.

Understanding communism

When one sets out to study economics, one often encounters a definition of the subject along these lines: "Economics is the study of how people choose to allocate scarce resources to achieve their unlimited desires." Not everyone in the world can live in a beachfront home, own a private jet and have maids do their laundry. And not everyone can have enough to eat, either. Especially if they like to eat the eggs of some endangered species.

That is the problem of scarcity. The essential challenge of any system of economics is therefore to reconcile the conflict between scarce resources and unlimited desires. In simplistic

Collective farmer, USSR, 1935 - 1940

terms, it would seem that we have the following choice: to muddle through with an inefficient system where some people have much more than they need while others not enough; or to attempt to perfect a system in which everyone has what they need, and possibly a bit more.

As we discussed in the previous chapter, in a capitalist system the conflicts generated by scarcity are resolved through the action of the profit motive, which acts as the reconciling force. There are a few winners and lots of losers, but theoretically, through competition, resources will be allocated efficiently (so as to maximize profits) and productive economic activity will be maximized. And while the benefits of this economic activity may be distributed in a very uneven fashion, everyone should feel wealthier over time, provided they continue to believe in the following cliché: "a rising tide lifts all boats."

A communist system takes a different approach. In order to solve the problem of scarcity, and to remedy the unfairness and inhumanness of the capitalist model, responsibility is relegated to a central planning entity to allocate productive resources and distribute goods and services on a purely rational basis, giving priority to needs rather than desires. This central planning entity assumes the role of the reconciling force, making decisions on how the system is managed. Instead of instituting and regulating a marketplace where goods and services are exchanged through trade, it institutes and regulates a centralized scheme for allocating the goods and services produced by all, for the benefit of all.

This all sounds reasonable enough, but as is the case with many things, there is a significant difference between theory and practice, and "the devil is in the details." Central planning has been shown to work rather well for capital goods, infrastructure, housing, human welfare and healthcare, education and quite a few other things; but it tends to fail when it comes to providing consumer products and services, fostering rapid technological innovation in fields such as computer engineering, and making a profit in international trade.

Communist theory

Western propaganda often presents communism as an evil force, and some would even go so far as to assert that any form of socialism (often used as a synonym for communism) is to be guarded against and purged from the world. At the superficial level of popular culture, this view is reinforced through films such as *Top Gun* and *Rocky IV*, in which rugged individualist mavericks (including a character actually named Maverick) lead the fight for the free world and liberty against cold, steely, menacing communists who inexplicably manage to thrive on tyranny and oppression.

But to consider communism in rational terms a slightly more in-depth analysis is required. Biased propaganda aside, it is a mode of operating that is common to us all—east and west, north and south—and in this chapter we shall seek to understand the flaws of communism as a political system, as well as the forces of cooperation which it can unleash given favorable circumstances, and which are natural and inherent in our nature.

Theoretically, communism aspires to fulfill the utilitarian creed of "the greatest good for the greatest number." The ideal is that each shall contribute according to their ability and that each shall receive according to their need, such that the common good is achieved. This is a simple theory and there are many examples of communist living arrangements that we can all relate to.

Within a family unit, family members contribute to the overall welfare and happiness of the household. Parents give freely to their children, and a husband and wife will generally share resources and work without keeping financial accounts against each other. Among friends and extended family we may give and receive with no expectation of remuneration, simply because some of us have a little more than the others and can afford to help out. When we join a sports club or some other voluntary organization we may take on work without any expectation of payment, but simply for the good of the other members or beneficiaries of that organization. Some can take on more than others, but in principle it is done with good will and freedom of heart, and it is also implicit and expected that some will benefit more than others.

At this level communist theory works remarkably well, and would be considered a natural part of a caring and functional society. When it is at its best, it may even be said that the motivating force behind it is love.

The communist model becomes less successful as soon as it is extended in scope beyond the number of people who know and care for each other. The greater the number of people involved, the greater is the complexity of the structures required to arrange and coordinate their activities, spawning a managerial class, creating gross inefficiencies, and culminating in the ultimate calamity that is the communist state with central planning for the masses and—since not everyone can be part of the managerial class—control by force.

Dunbar's number

The relationship between scale and the problems associated with communal arrangements is in large part explained by the theory of contemporary evolutionary biologist Robin Dunbar, who proposes a limit to the number of people with whom one can maintain stable social relationships. This number, known as Dunbar's number, has been proposed to lie between 100 and 250 people, with a commonly used value of 150, which turns out to be rather ubiquitous: it is the average size of a village, from neolithic through medieval times, the average size of a clan of hunter-gatherers in prehistory, and a common unit size of professional armies.

The observation is quite intuitive because there are numerous such contexts to which we can all immediately relate. In a business, for example, 150 people is about the approximate staff number beyond which additional rules and layers of management need to be created in order to run it effectually.

Dunbar's number can be recognized as a common-sense observation. It can also be seen as a profound and simple theory that explains much about humanity. In Dunbar's analysis, the tendency of humans to form cohesive and cooperative social networks of up to approximately 150 people is not just a quirk of human nature but an essential part of it—one which we can only neglect at our own peril. What Dunbar offers is nothing less than an explanation of how we came to be and who we are.

Robin Dunbar

All animals, our good selves included, don't survive willy-nilly; they have a strategy that enables them to survive. Spiny, poisonous fish survive by being spiny and poisonous: try to eat one and you die in great pain. Great white sharks survive by being the largest and most dangerous predators in the sea. We, on the other hand, lacking poisonous spines, razor-sharp teeth or even fur, manage to survive by establishing cooperative groups: we band together, we communicate effectively using language, and we use our wits to fight off larger animals, acquire resources and protect each other. This is what our species is, what it did for most of its history (up until the relatively recent development of towns and city-states), and what it still must do today, albeit in slightly different ways.

It certainly helped the human evolutionary cause that we became upright and bipedal, evolved opposable thumbs and developed an intelligence sufficient to make tools and capture fire. But the thing most fundamentally responsible for our means of survival and advancement was our behavior as groups, including language and the complex patterns of social interaction that make up and sustain a diversity of cultures—each uniquely adapted to its environment. It is not by chance that, deprived of such a naturally close-knit group, so many of our young people now plug themselves into social media and form networks of largely superficial, electronically mediated substitutes for

A Shoshone tipi encampment, Wyoming, 1870

belonging and interaction. It is a consequence of their nature, which has evolved for sociability and the establishment of groups that care about and look out for their members.

Humans as a cooperative and a competitive species

The observation that humans are by nature and adaptation a cooperative species was explored at length by the Russian scientist Peter Kropotkin, whose most renowned work is *Mutual Aid: A Factor of Evolution.* He wrote in support of communist modes of organization, and made many observations about how these were more natural and efficient for both production and consumption than capitalist ones.

Peter Kropotkin

Like Darwin, Kropotkin was a keen observer of nature. One of his favorite species was the ant. He observed that in an ant colony any one ant will always share its food "already swallowed and partly digested" with every member of the community which may ask for it, that they will sacrifice their own lives readily to save their larvae, and that they work constantly to build nests and store food, all for the collective good. In a colony of ants he saw a perfectly operating system of selfless industrious effort for mutual benefit.

Homesteaders, Nebraska, 1866

Turning to humans, he studied the success of various groups of immigrants to the United States, which, up until the nineteenth century, was still a pioneering country, and full of communist experiments of all kinds. As colonization proceeded westward, those who chose to be homesteaders and farmers in the emerging nation-state faced the challenge of surviving in a wilderness that lacked any established infrastructure. This context provided rich material for the analysis of group interaction, and it was Kropotkin's unambiguous conclusion that those groups that set themselves up along communist lines—sharing tools, pooling labor, establishing communal reserves of food and fodder for lean times, and building infrastructure that all could use—far outperformed those that tried to make a go of it as individuals or families. But once the groups managed to generate some surplus wealth, making the imperative of survival less important, and also perhaps being

69

Charles Darwin

influenced by the norms of surrounding society, they tended to revert to the use of private property.

In presenting numerous examples of communist success, Kropotkin challenged the view of social Darwinists, who believed that conflict between groups in society leads to social progress. His view was that it is patterns of cooperation that are central to the survival of a species, and he rejected the idea that competition within a species stimulated evolutionary vigor to any significant extent. Kropotkin argued that science does not suggest that humans will always look out for "number one," and that in nature it is selfless action that predominates within groups, while the path of unabated selfishness tends to end quickly in extinction.

The reconciling force behind communism

And so, the natural tendency of humans to want to cooperate and organize along communist lines is innate. But then why has the failure of communism as a political system been so profound?

The problem is scale! When communist arrangements extend beyond a group of people who know each other, a hierarchy becomes necessary, at which point the reconciling force changes. In a hierarchy the authority for making decisions is assigned to those at the top, and without a well-developed system of self-regulation that allows for feedback from below, the primary reconciling force then becomes **reason of the rulers**.

This scheme sounds harmless enough, but it has a fundamental flaw: it depends on the high quality of the rulers, and, as history has proven, this is somewhat problematic, because benevolent and competent rulers happen more or less by accident, while weak, corrupt and incompetent rulers appear quite regularly. The examples of this process are legion, and many countries have cycled endlessly from being governed by a benevolent and competent ruler, then by his weak, corrupt and incompetent successors (often his own children), then collapsing through chaos, internal conflict or invasion, before finally, if they are lucky, moving on to the next benevolent and competent ruler.

In expanding our understanding of the way reason of the rulers acts as the reconciling force, and how this is problematic for large societies, it is useful to distinguish between the two types of communism loosely distinguished above, which could be described as **personal communism**—relating to groups of up to 150 people, and **impersonal communism**—relating to groups larger than 150 people. For the great majority of human existence, personal communism has been the system that we have lived by, whereas impersonal communism was a short-lived 20th-century experiment.

In personal communism the motivating force of the rulers is more strongly aligned with the welfare of the group they rule, because they are personally connected to them in very real, familial ways. The decisions of the rulers are usually made in a setting that resembles a family reunion or a tribal council. There is plenty of opportunity for direct participatory democracy, where all members of the group have a say in the decision-making process. This type of decision-making also tends to be self-regulating, because its effects are seen and felt by the rulers, and because its benefits are shared on a relatively equal basis. The village chief, for example, has an incentive to be very careful in making his decisions because, should they impinge upon his mother-in-law, he would never hear the end of it.

In impersonal communism the leaders are only somewhat connected to the communities which they govern. The larger the system they oversee, the less self-regulating their decision-making becomes. The ultimate disconnect occurred when Chairman Mao was able to rule over nearly a billion people, having scant real exposure to the suffering he caused through his grandiose, madcap schemes for rapidly modernizing China. Carving large irrigation canals through mountains using picks and buckets was a bad idea, but people were afraid to tell him that, plus he didn't care. Through his actions tens of millions of people starved to death. But neither he, nor Joseph Stalin, who caused similar suffering in Russia, were ever in the same house as one of their subjects, who had skin hanging from their bones, eating mud and leaves and tearfully watching their children slowly die from lack of food. They lived in palaces and had plenty to eat.

Thus, at a large enough scale, communism is certainly no better, and possibly even worse, than capitalism, which has also been responsible for its fair share of genocidal bouts of starvation, when those who had wealth

Russian Famine, Saratov, 1921

and power callously neglected the needs of others. In the case of the potato famine in Ireland, a million people starved in a country rich with agricultural land surrounded by a sea full of fish, due to what was essentially an act of economic subversion designed to destroy Irish society. At the time, most of the good land in Ireland was owned by British absentee landlords, who extracted an income from the local population through taxation and rent, and who, even when facing large-scale death among their tenants, sought to protect their income. In particular, they opposed aid to the starving farmers on the grounds that this would reduce their incentive to work, and they continued to collect rents and evict those who could not pay throughout the famine, perhaps thinking that the troublesome Irish would feign starvation every year if they thought they could get away with not paying their dues. Throughout the period of the famine more than enough food was produced within the country to feed all of its residents, and huge quantities of it were exported.

The problem with communist leaders

Joseph Stalin

Mao Tse Tung

Pol Pot

Kim Il-sung

A communist government is neither a necessary nor a sufficient condition for bringing about horrific suffering and genocide: the Irish famine did not require a communist government, nor did Germany under Hitler. But several communist leaders have become infamous for the suffering they imposed upon their people. Joseph Stalin—paranoid, maniacal and totally without conscience—was responsible for the deaths of an estimated 20 million people; Mao Tse Tung brought about the deaths of an estimated 45 million people; Kim Il-sung, the founder of the People's Republic of Korea, is blamed for 1.6 million deaths; and Pol Pot, who oversaw the genocide in the killing fields of Cambodia, is estimated to have taken more than a million lives.

Lord Acton

As historian Lord Acton famously said, "Power tends to corrupt, and absolute power corrupts absolutely." Each of these four men has proven this to be true: Stalin, Mao, Il-sung and Pol Pot all rose to power as populist revolutionaries offering a vision of hope to their followers. When they first came to power, each of them headed up a people's movement and enjoyed a great deal of optimistic public support. But the power that was entrusted to them, amplified by their psychopathic tendencies and their lack of conscience, allowed them to take their people down a very dark path.

The story of this particular human frailty—of the moral weakness of those in possession of power—is powerfully parodied in George Orwell's allegorical novel, *Animal Farm*. The story is set on a farm run by one Mr. Jones—a heavy drinker who does not feed or take care of his animals. The animals band together and revolt, driving Mr. Jones from the farm and committing to run the farm themselves together, for the mutual benefit of all. In taking over the farm, they adopt the Seven Commandments of Animalism, including the decree that "all animals are equal," and as they work cooperatively, unimpeded by the selfish exploitation of their former master, things become better for a while. But eventually the pigs, who were the leaders of the animal rebellion, start to assume more authority. The spirit of equality declines and, as the situation degenerates, the pigs eventually come to use the dogs to keep the rest of the animals in line. They also start to wear clothes, walk upright, drink alcohol and use whips. In essence, they became indistinguishable from the human master they overthrew. In the process, the Seven Commandments of Animalism were replaced with just one: "All animals are equal, but some animals are more equal than others."

This is the scenario that has played out in most of the experiments with nation-state communism. In China, the ruling Communists, have now become almost indistinguishable from the imperial capitalists they once overthrew. Mao, at his victory speech in Tiananmen Square, proclaimed that China would become free from inequality and foreign domination. But now his granddaughter, Kong Dongmei, is a successful entrepreneur and property owner whose personal fortune is estimated at $815 million at the time of writing—an outrageous example of inequality in a country where much of the population lives on less than $2 per day. In the meantime, the Chinese government, which once violently overthrew its colonial masters, has come to dominate large parts of Africa and other parts of the developing world. This hypocritical about-face took place in the span of only 60 years.

The problem with people

It is not just the leaders that are problematic within the large-scale impersonal communist model. Ostensibly, it would seem that the general mass of people is also unsuited to such a setup.

In examining communism, we have confronted the problem of scarcity. Solving it requires the establishment of some system for allocating resources, which, in order to be effective, requires people to cooperate. But, just as with kindergarten children working out how to share toys, there arises the issue of fairness. Except that the adults aren't playing—they are deadly serious, because they need the resources in order to survive. Fairness then becomes something of an unattainable ideal, because someone inevitably has to give up more than the others. Some are less predisposed to giving than others and try to shirk their responsibilities. Bullies are always lurking in the background, ready to dominate and take more than their share.

To keep the peace, something more substantial than spontaneous cooperation must be brought to bear. In the case of kindergartners unable to share toys, the presence of an adult is usually enough to provide the needed mediating influence. But when it comes to the serious business of mediating the sharing of essential resources among adult strangers, the task of mediation becomes significantly more fraught.

The main obstacle to the implementation of an equitable and intelligent system of resource allocation and sharing among strangers is human nature itself. When given the responsibility to make intelligent, rational and impartial decisions on behalf of others, there are not many who prove to be up to the task. When such leadership roles come with some amount of arbitrary authority, they attract those who are predisposed to co-opting them—to indulge of their whims and fancies, or to test their pet theories of social organization.

At the same time, ordinary people, not endowed with any special authority, often need some sort of external system of control to keep them honest. One of the key differences between capitalism and communism is in how they impose discipline on people.

Discipline

In the capitalist system discipline is imposed by the markets. A multitude of

The Sword of Damocles

77

businesses, of their own initiative, produce goods and services for sale in the marketplace. If they can't sell enough to cover their costs, they lose money. If they lose enough money, they go bankrupt and liquidate, taking much of the investment capital of the owners with them. This Sword of Damocles hangs over them, ever ready to decapitate them should they make bad decisions or allow themselves to become inefficient. The imperative of profit imposes external discipline on businesses and, indirectly through their managers, on their employees.

In a communist system, decisions on what to produce and how much of it to produce are made by central planners. They try and take an overview of the entire economic system, evaluating available resources and needs, then organizing the production of the goods and services as required. This is a very complex task, covering everything from making shoes to building airplanes, and requiring the programming and coordination of a huge number of inputs and outputs distributed across numerous locations and organizations. Within the central planning system, accountability comes from a different source than in the capitalist, market-driven model: instead of there being a multitude of small entities fighting for survival, there is a single large state entity, with many departments, making decisions on behalf of everyone.

Inherent in this system of management by bureaucracy on a very large scale is the dissipation of political discipline imposed from outside. Missing are the marketplace to set prices, the precise measuring stick of profit or loss, and the imminent threat of failure due to lack of profit. Without them, performance measures tend to become arbitrary and the consequences of failure are attenuated by social pressures to keep people employed. Whatever discipline can be imposed is determined within the bureaucracy itself, and in essence can only be imposed by one part of the same bureaucracy on another. Since bureaucratic organizations inevitably strive to protect themselves and their own interests, such disciplinary actions tend to be limited in scope.

The central planning system lacks many things: the self-regulating mechanisms of a market economy with its many feedback loops, the ultimate accountability for profits and losses and the automatic punishment of bad decisions and poor results, and the automatic positive reinforcement of innovation and successful risk-taking. Their lack can be compensated in just one way: by creating a superior, supremely effective, incorruptible bureaucratic organization—a tall order indeed!

This leads to the main critique of impersonal communism: that it cannot work because people are generally not up to the task of making it work. Centrally planned economies can produce good results for a time—either because of external pressures or because of a wave of enthusiasm. During World War II, for example, the US economy was centrally planned—with the production of automobiles banned, gasoline rationed, and most productive resources redirected toward defense—and this, along with a huge resource base, is what helped produce a victory for the Allies. After the Revolution of 1917, having overthrown a corrupt, incompetent, racist and antisemitic aristocracy, the USSR surfed on a wave of popular enthusiasm, leading to rapid industrialization, urbanization and a dramatic increase in the standard of living—much of which occurred while the US was wallowing in the Great Depression.

But such positive effects are temporary. Without the fear of failure and the pressure to succeed imposed by the ruthless market, the imperative for good, efficient work inevitably diminishes over time, initiating a slide toward ineffectualness, indolence and irresponsibility. It is a slippery slope that terminates in a culture of long lunches, pretending to be busy, padding production numbers, not taking any risks, not rocking the boat, and staying the course. The economy gradually decays into a wasteful, dysfunctional torpor. Sometimes the leaders find a way to freshen up the system, usually through violent purges, but these, unsurprisingly, tend to produce mixed results: the positive short-term effects on productivity are balanced by the negative long-term effects on social well-being, cohesion and morale.

Marxism

To complete our assessment of communism, we must give some consideration to Marxism. It could be said that Marxism is a fundamentally flawed philosophy. From an emotional point of view, it is insentient, materialistic and lacking compassion. From a political point of view, all attempts at its implementation have eventually failed.

But we should not denigrate it entirely, because Karl Marx's ideas arose from a noble impulse to ease the suffering of humanity and to improve the lot of the poor. Marx observed the terrible exploitation of workers in European factories in the midst of the industrial revolution. He then went to great lengths to catalogue the privations he observed—of the thousands of children working 12 hours a day, seven days a week, in dark cold factories, driven deaf by machinery, maimed by dangerous equipment, breathing fibrous dust which destroyed their lungs, earning only enough to get a meager ration of food, sheltering in cold, squalid ghettos filled with sickness and misery. He was repulsed by what he observed and envisaged a different system where the workers would be empowered and not exploited. It is little wonder that Marx's ideas resonated with a great majority of the poorly treated industrial workers of the time.

But if we separate Marx's thinking into three categories—analytical, prescriptive and predictive—we find that only one of them has any great merit. His analysis of capitalism's failings is to this day light-years ahead of most of what is produced by contemporary economists. In essence, Marx is required reading for anyone who wants to understand capitalism. But the prescriptive elements of his thinking—on how an economy should be structured—can hardly be called a complete success. Yes, it was Marx's thinking that in large measure inspired China and Russia, among others, to throw off the yoke of Western imperialist exploitation and to emerge as powerful sovereign states, but now that they have done so they have found Marx's ideas to be rather beside the point in moving forward. Likewise, his pre-

Karl Marx

dictive thinking—of humanity's inexorable march toward a great global socialist proletarian revolution, culminating in the building of world communism—now produces little more than a sad chuckle from even the most hardcore Marxists.

But Marx's enduring appeal is not limited to the industrial proletariat who have nothing to lose but their chains, or to emerging post-colonial societies throwing off the yoke of imperialist exploitation. Another of Marx's key contributions to the study of economics was his realization that capitalism creates alienation, because workers lose control of their lives when they lose control of their work. This creates an existential crisis: as workers cease to feel that they are autonomous beings living useful lives, people's lives lose their meaning. Marx was right: In Gallup's 2013 State of the American Workplace study, 70% of the participants described themselves as "disengaged" from their work.

Negativity begets negativity

Given the many failings of the communist nation-state—its propensity to install megalomaniac leaders, its lack of the self-regulating features of the marketplace, and its failure to produce goods and services in sufficient abundance to provide for a reasonable standard of living—the logical conclusion is that capitalism is superior to communism. Indeed, capitalism has been shown to provide a materially better standard of living for a larger number of people, while communism has been largely abandoned.

But while capitalism has brought us a long way in improving the material quality of our lives, this progress has been attained at a cost, and, just as with the great successes of communism, the gains will prove to be temporary. Like a virulent form of cancer that consumes its host, the eventual outcome will be lethal if it is allowed to carry on unchecked. Negativity begets negativity, and, as we summarized in the previous chapter, a system that has selfishness, fear and greed at its core cannot be fixed—it must be supplanted.

The failure of most of the experiments in building communism at the scale of the nation-state in part explains the apathetic response to the ills of capitalism. If communism is the only alternative, but can be quickly dismissed, then none of us is able to paint a picture of anything better. It does not help that most of the communist regimes we know of were founded on the basis of violent revolution, where one group has imposed its will over another with the threat of violent punishment for dissent. This also sets up a dynamic which is negative at its core, and, as a result, in our collective consciousness communism is not a term that inspires.

But as we discussed in this chapter, socialistic modes of living are at the core of what it means to be human. Working in a cooperative, good-hearted and reasonable way is what is healthy for the human spirit, and furthers the aspirational values of love, compassion and selflessness. These are all qualities that are associated with family and community, but which, as John Steinbeck suggested, are in-

John Steinbeck

versely cultivated in the capitalist system:

"The things we admire in men, kindness and generosity, openness, honesty, understanding and feeling are the concomitants of failure in our system. And those traits we detest, sharpness, greed, acquisitiveness, meanness, egotism and self-interest are the traits of success. And while men admire the quality of the first they love the produce of the second."

We cannot ignore that socialistic modes of living have been to our evolutionary advantage as a species, and are still a powerful force. If we are to rise to the challenges we collectively face, hope must rest in the idea that we can move closer toward a mode of living that embodies this spirit. Communism, in the way that most of us generally know it, is certainly not the answer. But it is still worthwhile to try and understand more about the spirit of people who have worked together cooperatively and successfully.

It is in our nature to want to live cooperatively, but it is in our culture to want to compete and to hoard. These problems with our culture are significant, and it is not realistic to expect that we can easily change our path. If an orchestra conductor were called upon to assemble a symphony orchestra out of musically untrained rabble, the music produced would sound rather awful. This is about where we are as a species in trying to make our way on the Earth. In our current stage of cultural development, we humans are not very good at harmonious living on a large scale. As a collective, we tend to be coarse, destructive and, based on the evidence, do not care what kind of world we are leaving to our children.

If there is to be a better way of organizing our society, the vibration of humanity must operate on a higher level. Great music is not made without effort and improvement. The ear must be trained, rhythm steadied and tone refined. The problem is not just in the systems we choose to employ to organize ourselves; the problem is also us.

5. Technology

Around mid-2005, I spent an afternoon with my grandmother, showing her how Skype worked. This made me realize what an interesting time she had lived through during her life. She was born in 1914 and had grown up on a small rural farm with no electricity, no car, no refrigerator, no television, no tractor and no phone. This was normal then. She lived in a prosperous country and was certainly not deprived by the standards of that time, but these technologies were still in their infancy and had not yet made their imprint. When she was a young girl, a trip to town had to be made by horse-drawn buggy and took a day. News from the other side of the world traveled on ships and took months. That the world had changed so much in her lifetime was something of a miracle. Who could have imagined so much?

She had arthritis in her hands, which she put down to milking cows for her father as a girl, when milking technology consisted of a stool and a bucket. By the time of her death

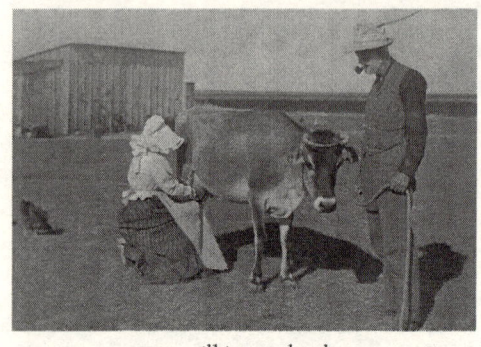
1920s milking technology

cows were being milked in robotic stalls, with the milk stored in large refrigerated vats, powered by electricity that came from the national grid. Large articulated trucks driving on paved roads collected the milk and delivered it to automated factories for processing. The milk products were sold via online auctions to bidders around the world, distributed to consumers by a global transportation network, and sold in supermarkets which stocked a variety and abundance of foods that a rural farm girl in the 1920s could not have possibly imagined.

Technology has been the dominant force for change in our modern world, and the pace of change has been exceptional. Never before in the history of humanity has our way of life been altered so quickly and so radically, and it would seem that the changes are far from finished.

Technology as a disruptive and creative force

A term that has come to be used widely in the internet-era business lexicon is market disruption. It describes innovation that occurs in a way that the market did not expect. A more precise term would be market annihilation—for a great many companies in sectors where the internet has changed the way we get things done are a shadow of their former selves or out of business entirely. Book publishers and sellers, typewriter manufacturers, newspapers, music recording companies, travel agencies and photography stores were some of the early casualties, but the list goes on and on.

Technology is relentlessly redefining commerce, and the power of computers—combining nearly effortless communication with huge processing power, and augmented by the potential of robotic automation—has the capacity to continue reshaping our society to a wondrous extent. Technologies such as driverless cars and trucks, 3D printing, decentralized energy generation and distribution, and advances in nanotechnology and biotechnology have the potential to drive the next wave of change. Just as 40 years ago we could not have conceived how profoundly the world would change with the advent of personal computers and the internet, it is now impossible to say what might lie ahead as these technologies cascade through the innovative and apparently unstoppable engine of human industry.[9]

Along with the advances in physical technology, a new social phenomenon has emerged, facilitated by the unprecedented options for connectedness and information sharing opened by information systems that span the globe. Contemporary social networks are just the beginning of what promises to be a thorough reshaping of the norms of social interaction. At present there is much that could be considered negative about this new regime. Previously respected boundaries relating to privacy and personal space have been eroded and

9 This assumes that our financial and economic system will remain stable.

human interaction via the medium of an electronic device is a poor substitute for real personal contact. The stimulation available through such devices has also fueled new types of addiction, resulting in many psychological strains and social distortions.

However, not all is negative in the rapid evolution of social-technical systems, and there is also evident a significant positive potential. There is much that is accessible to educate people, to inform them of different points of view and to connect them in ways not previously possible. Interestingly, all are also now susceptible to having their foibles filmed and distributed on a permanent record, which must surely also result in altered patterns of behavior and cultural adjustments toward how such transgressions are processed.

Because of these changes in the channels by which information is distributed, establishment narratives that have shaped popular opinion can now be effectively challenged by the public itself,

Russell Brand hosting The Trews

because anyone can now create and share media content globally. For example, comedian and political activist Russell Brand, in reaction to the inadequacy of the media as he saw it, decided to start his own news daily news program, called "The Trews." With no special technology and almost no investment or preparation, he was able to start producing his show, making it available to a worldwide audience usually in excess of 100,000 people per day.

This change is not occurring in accordance with any sort of plan, and we do not really know where it is leading us. But it does seem that there are three clear trends that can be observed:

1. The scarcity of basic goods and services is being reduced as the use of technology is making it easier to provide for the basic necessities of life for all.[10]

2. Technology is further undermining the structures that support our current debt-based economic system, leading us further toward a systemic crisis of capitalism.

3. The potential for reflexive and self-organizing structures is now much greater than it has ever been, making possible a new way of doing things.

Technology and scarcity

The renowned economist and social theorist Jeremy Rifkin believes that there is a major shift underway toward what he describes as a "zero marginal cost" economy, facilitated by the internet and the emergence of renewable energy technologies.

Jeremy Rifkin

---

10   Granted, this statement is a little simplistic in an overall context of resource depletion. For example, phosphate fertilizer is in limited supply.

Zero marginal cost describes a situation where it costs nothing to produce an extra unit of production. For example, if you are producing a new medicine it may cost many millions of dollars to do the research to come up with the formulation, test it and bring it to market. But once all of these expenses are paid for, it does not cost very much at all to produce the actual medicine, especially with modern automated factories—as little as a few cents per pill. Similarly, it may cost a recording company a lot of money to make a new album, but now that music can be copied and transmitted digitally the cost of producing extra copies of the album is essentially zero.

When the marginal cost of production tends toward zero, it becomes very difficult to maintain a sustainable business model because the product can no longer be kept scarce enough to command a high enough price to make a profit. If everyone can reproduce your product almost for free, then why would they pay for it? Copyright enforcement and appealing to the conscience of consumers only goes so far, especially when there are so many who are cynical about business. This challenge is especially acute for media businesses, whose products—such as newspapers, movies and books—can all be copied and distributed at close to zero cost.

Many other service industries are also being transformed by this dynamic. Who needs a travel agent when you can book online? Who needs a bank branch when you can do all your banking online? Who needs a shop, when you can buy your shoes, books and just about everything else you need from online retailers which have a tiny staff that coordinates the work of robots? Who needs a supermarket attendant when you can scan, pack and pay for your supplies yourself? Who needs a postal service when you can use email? Who needs a taxi driver when the car can drive itself? The list goes on and on, and the number of occupations and business models susceptible to technological obsolescence continues to increase.

Manufacturing has already gone through a similar process of marginal cost deflation since the advent of mass production, and many consumer goods continue to get cheaper as technology advances. Cars are made in gigantic factories in which robots work the assembly lines once operated by many thousands of men and women. Electronic items are made under similar conditions, with the result that a high-definition flat screen television now costs far less than the bulky cathode ray tube-based ones that were available thirty years ago.

Ford assembly line, 1913

Ford assembly line, 2014

It is now often the case that the biggest expenses in bringing a product to market are the licensing, marketing, distribution and retailing costs—not production costs. And even some of these costs, which provide little value to the end user, are being bypassed using modern means such as open source engineering and viral marketing using social media, further reducing the cost of goods.

The business of food production, which underwent a technological revolution some time ago, also continues to be redefined. Where the majority of the world's population once labored to produce enough food to eat, large machines and automated processes now do most of the work.

It is therefore not too much of a stretch to say that the problem of scarcity continues to exist in the modern world only because of the sophistication of our tastes. If we were to orient ourselves around the production of the basics required for a reasonable quality of life—food, shelter, transportation and a set of essential household items—modern production methods could easily provide enough for all.

Technology as a destabilizing force in a growth-oriented economy

New technology is often an economic game-changer because it significantly affects the dynamics of supply and demand, shifting them, often dramatically, to a new point of equilibrium. On the supply side of the equation, new technology often makes it very difficult for a business to continue operating profitably by making it possible to replace or replicate their products or services at a significantly lower cost. For instance, someone who once made his living repairing toasters is no longer in business, because it now costs less to buy a new toaster than to repair an old one. This happened because efficiency improvements in the manufacturing of toasters have made them both much cheaper (and much less maintainable), and their scarcity value has been greatly reduced.

For businesses which rely on intellectual property rights and brand recognition for their income, their business models are also being seriously challenged. The scarcity value of their products is maintained only through monopoly pricing, made possible by enforcing a monopoly on a design or a concept. When it becomes straightforward to reproduce licensed products, the quality gap between branded and alternative off-brand products vanishes, and it becomes very difficult for the originators of the design or the concept to maintain their market share.

The collaborative commons

An increasing number of designs and products is being created and distributed free of charge, and this also challenges established business models. Increasing amounts of high-quality digital content, design templates and open source computer software are being produced on a collaborative and voluntary basis, with the intention that they be shared for free. They have no scarcity value at all, making it very difficult to compete with them.

Wikipedia is the most well-known example of the "collaborative commons"—one that has become a global institution. Once upon a time Encyclopedia Britannica paid a well-educated staff a lot of money to write and update articles on information useful to the general public. But now tens of thousands of people do this for free in 291 languages on a range of topics far broader than a private company could ever have achieved. Another striking example is the Linux operating system, which started out as a hobbyist's toy, but is now the mainstay of data centers and supercomputers. It has achieved superior quality by allowing anyone who wants to dive into the computer code and find and fix defects or add features to do so—something that "closed source" systems such as Microsoft's make impossible.

One step removed from the collaborative commons is the decentralized and democratic marketplace, in which the interconnectedness of people is facilitating new ways of doing business that entirely bypass most large corporate players. Kickstarter and Indiegogo in finance, Airbnb in accommodation, eBay in retail and marketing, Über in transportation, blogging in news and entertainment and Craigslist for just about everything are but a few of the examples.

Emergent new attitudes

Businesses are also being affected by new attitudes that develop as new technology pervades society. There is a shift toward voluntary simplicity, where quality is favored over quantity. Steve Jobs, a trendsetter, famously always wore the same outfit and kept a spartan house, obsessed as he was with clearing away clutter and eliminating unnecessary junk.

Steve Jobs

In turn, we are witnessing a move by younger people toward embracing the concept that less is more. So long as they have a mobile phone, roof over their heads, clothes to wear and food to eat, this seems to satisfy most of their material needs. The crumbling economy has denied many of them the ability to own property or to achieve the security of a well-paid middle-class lifestyle. In response, they are accepting that there is a compromise to be made, where a lifestyle that is light on possessions and absent the full suite of material accoutrements, but, for many, also light on unwelcome, oppressive responsibilities, can be made satisfactory. This is something that has become increasingly apparent to car manufacturers, who have witnessed a decrease in the number of young people obtaining driver's licenses, along with steadily decreasing rates of car ownership by people under 30.

Along with these cultural shifts there is emerging a new understanding of how it may be possible to make one's life more compatible with sustainable living. There are now two generations who have grown up being educated about environmental issues, and who care about the environmental effects of their actions and of those of their leaders. Treading light on the earth has become an aspirational value of great significance to many people. This is also a force that is at work against the economic model of ever-expanding consumerist consumption, steadily shrinking the number of opportunities to make a profit by applying this model.

A challenge to the status quo

All around us we can plainly see that status quo capitalism is being seriously disrupted by new technology—and not as a result of any external action.

But to what effect?

One may contend that this new regime of ever-advancing disruptive technology can coexist peacefully with the status quo capitalist model. However, upon thinking it through, such speculation begins to sound increasingly outlandish. Our current growth-based economic model is entirely dependent on continuous growth in consumer spending, resulting in ever-increasing volumes of trade (in monetary terms) and ever-increasing incomes (to be able to pay for these higher volumes of trade). In turn, these are predicated on ever-increasing levels of paid employment. Note, however, that none of these requirements is compatible with the trends just described.

The scenario faced by the music industry, to take a specific example, is being faced by other sectors of the world economy, albeit to different degrees. Thanks to new technology, no money is now required for the exchange of music, and hardly anyone needs to be employed in facilitating this exchange. It therefore contributes nothing to economic growth. In fact, its effect is the exact opposite: an economic contraction. As the economy steadily shrinks, the amount of money in circulation decreases, making it more difficult to service existing debt, creating a major headache for a financial system in which all money is created as debt.

For the time being, the building-out of this new world of technology, as developing countries catch up and, in certain cases, surpass the developed ones, seems to be able to offset the deflationary effect of new technology. But should this turn out to be a temporary effect, new technology will prove to be yet another force that is bringing us closer to the capitalist endgame.

This is all enough to drive a dyed-in-the-wool capitalist to despondency, but there are also reasons to be hopeful that in the falling away of the old there is a powerful latent potential for developing something positive and new.

6. Human Nature

Whenever we turn on the television news, we are presented with a tableau of brutality: war, murder, rape, theft, deceit, injustice, poverty, and waste. Turning back to our daily lives, we can see that ordinary people often find it hard to get along, to meet in the middle and carry on. We all have experiences which test our faith in humanity. How can we ever expect any sort of positive system for reconciling our differences to prevail in a world afflicted with so much strife?

It seems that there are always those who are ready to spoil whatever we set up, and who must be controlled with strict rules and the threat of punishment. And if something positive is set up that involves any sort of subtlety or complexity, then there are always those who—being clumsy and ignorant—are

Nuremberg rally, 1936

ready to lay waste to what has been initiated.

Always there are a few psychopaths among us. Completely self-interested and without compassion, they camouflage themselves using a well-socialized persona. They make friends and use fine words, but they are profoundly insincere. In a tight spot, they will only look out for themselves. How can we ever account for them in any alternative system?

And then there are those who conform to the norms of so-ciety, but who, given half a chance, will pick up a weapon and kill hundreds of innocent people in the name of some flimsy notion of righteousness. An ordinary person can quickly be put under the spell of groupthink, and be prompted to engage in all sorts of doubtful behaviors without coercion.

In a world of reasonable people

Everything would be so easy—if only people were reasonable!

Our current system is incredibly wasteful. But it is easy to envisage a plethora of things that could be done to improve our lot with just a bit of organization and consideration. So much of the Earth's resources are worthlessly squandered generating goods and services that are not really needed, that are produced inefficiently, or that are only marginally useful. If everyone could get along, and an intelligent, efficient, practical order prevailed, and resources could be conserved and allocated logically to produce useful things for people, there would be no need for a great many professions, which are themselves a sort of waste—of our time on Earth.

War, security, police and justice

For a start, most of the work associated with the military, police, security, legal and prison services would not be required—if only there were no need to stop people from fighting... if only nation states did not threaten each other with war and spend such an inordinate amount of money and time arming themselves and working out new ways to kill and dominate! That would immediately free up an abundance of resources.

For example, before the recent British election there was a debate as to whether the UK Government should replace their four aging nuclear submarines at a cost of £100 billion. Alternative ways proposed for spending such a large amount of money included fully funding 150,000 nurses and teachers for 30 years, building 1.5 million new homes, or scrapping student tuition fees for the next 30 years.

These and many other cost savings are obvious—provided we lived in a world of reasonable people who were always peaceful and considerate of oth-

Trident nuclear submarine

ers, and who never need to be opposed militarily, policed or put in prison. They would never blow up planes, rob each other at gunpoint, vandalize property or start riots. Now, wouldn't that be lovely?

A consumer society

If our value system were to change from one of conspicuous consumption to one of conservation and utility—as it mostly was up until the twentieth century—the quantity of goods that needs to be produced would be vastly reduced. At present, it is culturally acceptable (and even encouraged) to throw away much of what we buy after very little use, mindlessly squandering the resources required to produce it. The success of the capitalist system depends on the ever-increasing trade of goods and services, and this makes it fundamentally anti-conservationist. The advent of mass production made it possible to produce goods much more cheaply and in much greater quantities than ever before, chewing through natural resources at an ever-increasing rate.

In a world of reasonable people we would instead find ways to enjoy the benefits of all this technology, but make it durable and long-lasting. We wouldn't need to pay to constantly replace it, and would be able to work fewer hours. But to maintain existing power structures and to service ever-expanding levels of debt we must maintain endless economic growth, and to drive demand we must coerce peoples' appetites into desiring ever more stuff.

This was already clearly understood early in the twentieth century, at a time when a set of technological leaps was occurring. Goods that had previously been produced by craftsmen and artisans on a bespoke basis using labor-intensive methods were now being mass-produced in factories, facilitated by electricity and new transportation and communication systems. A 19th-century worker, for example, may have owned two sets of durable clothes that lasted him many years, one for daily living and the other for church and special occasions. Once it was possible to easily produce clothes through mass production, demand on the level of simple utility could be easily satisfied. The industrialist leaders of the time, recognizing that their factories would become idle as the new methods of production could produce far more goods than had previously been necessary, deliberately orchestrated a shift toward emotive consumption and away from practical utility to ensure that there would continue to be a market for their goods.

Paul Mazur, a leading Wall Street banker who once worked for the now infamously defunct Lehman Brothers, strategized in 1927: "We must shift America from a needs to desires culture. People must be trained to desire, to want new things, even before the old have been entirely consumed. ... Man's desires must overshadow his needs." And so they did: with the help of psychologists working with advertisers to exploit the foibles in peoples' subconscious minds—insecurity, lust and other such primal instincts—the consumption culture was born. With the consumption culture automatically came the plentiful waste generated by the production of throwaway goods designed for planned obsolescence.

Oscar Wilde

Within the consumption culture, all culture became reoriented toward consumption: formerly meaningful cultural festivals and rituals were commercialized—turned into reasons to go shopping for gifts (which are rarely all that useful). Fashion—which Oscar Wilde described as that which is so ugly that we have to change it every six months—came to permeate not just the clothing industry, but everything, from consumer electronics to furniture and interior décor. Fashion is purely arbitrary. A more reasonable and enlightened system would allow people to value durability and thrift, and to find meaningful, artful ways of expressing their individuality instead of following the lead of vapid advertisers and marketers. It is, after all, quite absurd to seek individual expression by following fashion, when that is mostly an unconscious, conformist response to advertisers implanting suggestions in the minds of the masses.

Wasting time

Numerous aspects of capitalism result in redundancy and duplication. For example, on my street there operate three removal companies that pick up garbage from different customers. This is justified by the theory that competition between the three companies drives efficiencies: to be efficient within a market economy, garbage removal operations have to be run in triplicate. But if the participants were reasonable and self-motivated they would find these efficiencies anyway, because picking up garbage inefficiently isn't a reasonable goal.

Here is another example of wasted time: when I worked for a local government authority there was a large office full of young, energetic and intelligent people processing permit applications and monitoring the actions of the citizens of the district. All of this would have been unnecessary if everyone obeyed this simple rule: "be reasonable to your neighbors, think of future generations, and do what your qualified consultants recommend as best practice to provide good outcomes." Instead, what they obey goes something like this: "Cut whatever corners you can, take all the advantage you can get away with, spend the least amount possible to maximize your profits, exploit technicalities in the wording of rules, beggar thy neighbor, and use fine words and obfuscation to try and get away with it all."

While I was working in this role, it became clear to me that a majority of citizens was reasonably ethical in the way they approached their affairs, but the self-interested approach of a minority made it necessary to maintain a huge system of rules and regulations, miring everyone in bureaucracy and distracting them with time-consuming tangential issues.

A large proportion of administration relates only to keeping accounts. It doesn't really contribute to the production of anything useful. In fact, the entire financial industry—lending, stock trading, banking and insurance—really just consists of people sitting at desks manipulating numbers in databases. Within the capitalist system, these professions are the enablers of the whole system of enterprise, and allow development and growth to occur. But if everyone was reasonable and did productive work according to what was required, they would also be mostly unnecessary.

Productivity correlates highly with motivation. In the current system, people who go through the motions of doing work, but are not really engaged in their jobs or working to their true capacity, generate a lot of waste. Their working conditions are often stifling, and require people to do repetitive, inane tasks, never able to complete anything to their satisfaction. As a result, many people feel frustrated in their work and produce only the minimum required. This is exacerbated by the educational system, which compartmentalizes people into narrowly defined functions, denying them the traditional fulfillment that comes with the self-sufficient mastery of a range of crafts.

In a system made up of reasonable people, work would be linked with positive outcomes for things that the workers care about. It would foster the development of skills and expertise in a stable setting with varied and fluid individual roles. This would empower people, improve job satisfaction, and significantly increase everyone's productivity.

Reasonable people would take on the burden of doing the work that is actually required, voluntarily and without complaint, knowing that they were doing their bit for the greater good—from which they would also benefit.

Only a fraction of the population is engaged in productive work

In the current capitalist model only a fraction of people actually work. The very rich are able to live off their investments and do not contribute to actual production. The very poor are excluded from production through structural unemployment which, in a capitalist economy, is considered healthy if it hovers around 5%. Sickness and disability, much of it the result of poor working conditions and overwork, which would not occur in a reasonable system, further reduce the pool of working people.

More resources are wasted in picking up the pieces, trying to mitigate the social consequences of the current system, which is too brutal, stressful and unhealthy for many people to handle. If people were reasonable, all the energy expended on social services, hospitals and pharmaceuticals in order to help masses of isolated, desperate and insecure people would be greatly reduced. The large administrative bureaucracy which serves to support this safety net would also be mostly unnecessary.

The useful uses of technology

Modern technology provides huge opportunities for the elimination of large amounts of waste. Given a more deliberate, targeted set of outcomes which are based on reasonableness, this could produce large benefits. Combined with a culture of conservation, instead of a culture of consumption, technology has great potential for solving problems. Producing enough clean energy to meet our requirements is one obvious example. Production technology has advanced to a point where a great variety of products can be produced at a low resource cost thanks to the use of automation and robotics and advances in materials science. It provides many opportunities for the expression of individual tastes and styles by producing customized goods.

In a reasonable system, it would not be possible to accumulate disproportionately large hoards of individual wealth. This would no doubt crimp the style of those who wish to express themselves in grand ways by cruising about in megayachts or by wearing a new pair of shoes every day, but in an enlightened setting, in which the individual hoarding of resources at the expense of others would be considered distasteful, such people would be few in number.

Such explorations into what a reasonable system would be like can be carried on ad infinitum. A case in point is the Zeitgeist Movement, which has become quite prolific and very detailed in their formulation of how things could be done differently. They advocate for a resource-based economy based on natural law (the laws of nature), free from private property and money, where competition is replaced by the wisdom of a computerized planning system. Central to their concept is the idea that technology can be used to transcend scarcity, creating an easily produced abundance of all the basic needs of human existence. Many of their ideas—such as growing large amounts of food in 30-story towers erected within city limits, or harnessing geothermal energy to satisfy the world's energy demands—sound far-fetched. But over the last 50 years we have witnessed again and again how many things previously thought far-fetched became feasible, then common, then available on a mass basis.

Human psychology

The problem with all of this is that people aren't all that rea-sonable.

Our motives are clouded by greed, fear, selfishness, lazi-ness, fecklessness, boredom, restlessness, vanity, lust and in-sincerity. They don't allow us to see ourselves clearly. We are all constantly involved in an internal dialogue of self-justifica-tion, attempting to convince ourselves of the value and rea-sonableness of our compulsions and urges. Each of us has at least a touch of such hazy thinking, and it prevents us from be-ing entirely reasonable.

But also within all of us are positive forces, in which our hope must be rooted. These qualities are the antidotes to the above, and include generosity, courage, sympathy, considera-tion, self-discipline, humility, respect, compassion, strength and sincerity.

Here is a folk story that has been circulated on the inter-net, of a man who has two wolves inside him:

An old man was teaching his grandson about life...

"A fight is going on inside me," he said to the boy. "It is a terrible fight and it is between two wolves. One is evil—he is anger, envy, sorrow, regret, greed, arrogance, self-pity, guilt, resentment, inferiority, lies, false pride, superiority, self-doubt, and ego. The other is good—he is joy, peace, love, hope, serenity, humility, kindness, benevolence, empathy, generos-ity, truth, compassion, and faith. This same fight is going on inside you—and inside every other person, too."

Two wolves

The grandson thought about it for a minute and then asked his grandfather: "Which wolf will win?"

The old man simply replied: "The one you feed."

This story, while a little trite, expresses the reality of our situation. By continuing to worship at the altar of the profit motive, we feed the "evil" wolf. But it is the "good" wolf that we must collectively feed if we are to set ourselves on a more positive path.

7. Addressing the Question of Motive

Every day presents us with choices between doing the right thing that is difficult and taking the easy way out. It would seem that taking the easy way out is almost a default setting, as if there were a powerful force pulling us away from anything that involves hard work.

It is easier to blame others than to hold yourself to account. It is easier to indulge in sensual pleasures, eating, drinking and sleeping, than to exercise self-control and to work steadily toward a good outcome. But we know that, in order to live a life that has some sort of purpose, we must make positive choices that require effort. All of us face the constant challenge of rising above our likes and dislikes, of foregoing immediate gratification for the sake of longer-term benefit, and it is a certainty in life that in order to be functioning human beings we must take responsibility and pull ourselves up by our own bootstraps. Our struggle begins at the act of conception, when a sperm battles against great odds to penetrate the egg. From that point on and until our last breath, the struggle continues.

Given our natures, we can be assured that no system of organizing people can avoid work, struggle and difficult interpersonal dynamics. Work and struggle underpin life itself. The choice we face is whether to work with some degree of self-awareness and purpose, or to submit to being prodded along by external forces that blindly herd us toward unconscious, unchosen conformity.

Thus, we cannot avoid struggle; but we can reframe the structure within which we struggle—and find a new way of operating, in which the goodness within us may be allowed to grow without being constantly beaten down by the inherent negative dynamics of our current, profit-driven system.

Reframing the struggle

In simple terms, we can approach the task of finding an alternative to the profit motive in the manner of an engineering design problem. The design parameters are as follows:

1. There must operate a reconciling force that is positive.
2. Simplicity of the overall system is a key requirement.
3. Incentives must align with respect for our environment.
4. There must be a capacity for dealing with negativity.
5. Democratic principles should be upheld, and centralization of power avoided.
6. Work and positive contribution should be incentivized.

It is certainly possible to add to this list, but these six points appear to be both necessary and sufficient: if any of these preconditions is not met, we can safely assume that the outcome will be failure.

A positive reconciling force

On the most basic level, human fallibility is regulated in two ways. The first is through fear, which motivates us to avoid negative outcomes. The second is through aspiration, which motivates us to achieve positive outcomes. A person may re-frain from stealing to avoid prison; another out of respect for others' property and a belief in the value of harmonious living. One day we may work because we need the money; the next because we want to contribute to something useful and worth-while. Aspects of both our baser and our better nature are al-ways at work, and both the carrot and the stick are needed in any system for organizing people.

One of the great strengths of the profit motive-driven sys-tem is that this carrot-and-stick dynamic is well-defined and robust. But this strength is also a weakness, for it contains a serious flaw: only a limited few can do well in chasing the car-rot of profit, while the remainder of the population, along with the environment, get the stick and become collateral damage. Anyone who can't make a profit is denied access to resources and is subjected to the depravity of war, poverty, bondage and defilement.

I therefore propose an alternative carrot-and-stick mech-anism, which is predicated on one important imperative: peo-ple must be firmly reconnected with the consequences of their actions. As chance would have it, there is a remarkable trans-formation happening in our culture at present, which is en-abling this exact thing. While many of us are not yet aware of its significance, I believe that it has huge potential.

The new ubiquity of mobile computing coupled with widespread internet access has made us potentially visible to the world in nearly all contexts—even in our bedrooms. We are becoming acutely aware of the dangers inherent in a situation in which privacy is disappearing, and of powerful entities with sinister, self-serving agendas that are able to monitor our every move. But there is also a very positive potential developing, and we should not lose sight of it.

In a world where all of our actions can to be recorded on video at any time, and the resultant video distributed for all to see in perpetuity, a brief descent into the red mist of anger may make us the star in an online viral hit, while a moment of ill-advised conduct may land us on the evening news. The world has become smaller and the channels of communication much broader. The filters of the establishment media and the limitations of the physical published word no longer apply, and almost anywhere we go we can be called to account using electronic evidence that can be distributed for all to see. The actions of a shoplifter may be caught on CCTV and posted to YouTube; a public official taking a bribe may be covertly filmed and shamed on Facebook; mendacious establishment narratives can be swiftly discredited by anyone with a phone, an internet connection and a more enlightened point of view. Thus, the "stick" of public scrutiny is evolving into something imbued with new power and vitality. This is happening naturally, without overt direction—and that is a hallmark of something that is resilient and robust. It may in due course provide an emergent new context for the development of a more moral society.

While views of morality can differ, the Golden Rule—"Do unto others as you would have them do unto you"—is something that almost all of us accept as natural and right. Applying it implies being considerate of others ahead of one's own narrow interests—while expecting others to reciprocate. It is this very dynamic that I propose as a

Thomas Paine

new reconciling force for our society. It is the ideal of selfless service—an ethic that embodies what must become the aspirational part of a new carrot-and-stick regime to live by. In a world where selfishness seems to reign supreme, this may sound like a utopian dream, but I contend that it is eminently achievable. Despite our current situation, almost all of us are able to relate to idea of a fair deal for others. The creation of the correct social context is all that is required for this reconciling force to become operative.

The system must be simple

Thomas Paine, an Enlightenment hero who was a champion of liberty and democracy, authored a pamphlet, *Common Sense*, on the nature of government, which was a source of inspiration for the American Revolution in the 1700s.

On simplicity, he wrote:

"I draw my idea of the form of government from a principle in nature, which no art can overturn, viz. that the more simple any thing is, the less liable it is to be disordered; and the easier repaired when disordered."

This is a true statement that applies in all areas. In general, it could be said that any system that is self-organizing in accordance with well-understood principles, and allows for individual failures without jeopardizing the whole, is more likely to be successful than one that requires complex structures of bureaucracy and administration. One of the fatal flaws of nation-state communism was its reliance on a top-down, monolithic organizational structure. The more bureaucracy there is, the more disenfranchised and disengaged is the ordinary person, and the less effective the system.

The cumbersome nature of bureaucracies, and their almost inevitable lack of reflexivity, is humorously described by Cyril Parkinson in his book *Parkinson's Law And Other Studies in Administration*. Parkinson spent much of his career working for the British Civil Service, and he observed that as Great Britain's overseas empire declined, the number of staff it employed increased, to a point where, farcically, just at the time when it was wound down due to a lack of colonies to administer, it employed more staff than it ever had before. This he attributed to two causes: first, that "An official wants to multiply subordinates, not rivals" and second, that, "Officials make work for each other." In accordance with these, he developed a light-hearted mathematical model of bureaucratic expansion, and concluded that the number employed in a bureaucracy rises by between "5.17 percent and 6.56 percent per year, irrespective of any variation in the amount of work (if any) to be done."

A similar situation can be observed in our current profit motive-driven system, where, with the advances in technology that have transformed food production, construction and manufacturing, never before has there been less work to do, yet never before have there been so many people busily engaged in

Cyril Parkinson

marginally useful work. Joseph Tainter, in his insightful tome *The Collapse of Complex Societies*, describes this phenomenon as the diminishing returns of increasing complexity.

Thus, if an alternative system is to be lasting and effective, it must avoid complexity and bureaucracy as much as possible.

Incentives must align with respect for our environment

We all know that one should avoid fouling one's nest. On a purely utilitarian level this seems common-sense. On another level it relates to living a dignified life: living in harmony with nature, apart from being an existential imperative, sets a respectful tone and is a hallmark of healthy living. At present, it's something that we are doing not at all well.

In seeking to understand why we are degrading the environment that sustains us, it is interesting to consider the role of our attitudes toward the Earth. At one end of the scale, many traditional cultures consider the Earth to be the Holy Mother, a beneficent giver of life. At the other extreme, most modern scientists consider it to be an agglomerated mass of gases and minerals where all life evolves by random chance.

The nature of the cultural relationship between us and the Earth has undoubtedly had an impact on the way that people have treated their environment, and it is interesting to consider how attitudes toward the Earth have evolved over time. Long ago, our Stone Age ancestors had an innate respect for the Earth, borne of their close contact with nature in their everyday life. This did not stop some of them from hunting various species to extinction, but mostly they were passive with respect to altering the Earth, living in harmony with its natural rhythms, aware of the subtleties of their environment that made their existence possible.

The Kalahari Bushmen, prior to colonization, were an example of this mode of living. They lived with few material possessions, and their impact on the land was slight. They had a rich culture built on their deep respect for nature. Because of their fellowship with the Earth they were able to survive in hostile environments, in which most people wouldn't last three days.

San Bushmen, Namibia

In the modern day, engineering and technology have led us toward an altogether different relationship with the Earth. We have assumed a far more active role and, through ingenuity and brute force, human systems have achieved some degree of superiority over the cycles of nature. Technology has separated everyday living from the processes that sustain life on Earth. Barren land can now be made verdant with chemical fertilizers and irrigation; meat no longer has to be chased down but arrives on supermarket shelves in small plastic packages; heating and air conditioning systems produce air at the same temperature regardless of the temperature outside. Such triumphs can't but introduce an element of arrogance into our attitudes toward natural systems.

City dwellers have particularly little contact with the elements that feed them, being cocooned away from the business end of Nature. This was startlingly brought into focus by a recent survey conducted

Supermarket meat counter

by the British Nutrition Foundation when it found that nearly a third of primary school children think that cheese comes from plants, that one in ten secondary school children believe that tomatoes grow under the ground, and nearly one in five primary school children said that fish fingers are made from chickens.

What's even worse, in the business world the relationship of a corporation with the Earth is completely impersonal. Boards of directors view the Earth as a strictly economic entity, with a value assessed by measures such as grams of metal per ton of rock, bushels of corn produced per acre of land, or calories of energy per kilogram of coal. The extent to which they exploit and degrade the Earth is limited only by limits to profitability and by legal regulations—an approach that is hopelessly one-dimensional. It summarily ignores the fact that the value of free ecosystem services that are being degraded—such as clean air, clean water and fertile land—is many times greater than the value generated by all human economic activity put together.

Matapo, a blind tohunga

Losing touch with nature is at the root of much of this confusion. When decision-makers become removed from the effects of their decisions, the chance for error increases. Thus, in any future system, the alienation of man from nature must be reversed.

In coming up with better ways of connecting people with their environment, it is interesting to consider how traditional cultures managed resources. The Maori people of New Zealand, for example, had a system where the *tohunga* (spiritual or expert advisor) would declare a *tapu* (spiritual restriction) to protect a certain resource. Examples included restrictions on collecting of shellfish from a particular beach for a year, on catching more fish than you can

120

eat, or on visiting the catchment of a valued source of fresh water. In this way, the local resources that provided sustenance to the people were protected and treated with a spiritual reverence. While the Maori were certainly not perfect in their custodianship of the environment[11], in the course of their societal evolution they developed a strong culture of guardianship and conservation (*kaitiakitanga*), which has become central to their identity.

In the modern day, we attempt to define "sustainability" in scientific terms. One tool for conceptualizing this process is The Natural Step, conceived of by Swedish scientist Karl-Henrik Robèrt, a medical doctor and cancer researcher. Robèrt's interest in environmental issues was stimulated by the similarities he observed between the human body as a living system and the natural world as a living system, which are both based on cycles of replenishment and renewal.[12] According to him, maintaining the health of the human body, as well as the health of the natural environment, requires that we stay within the limits of these cycles of replenishment. Putting stress on the cycle of cell regeneration in the human body can cause cancer, while stressing the cycles of regeneration in nature can cause ecosystem collapse. In accordance with this general principle, Robèrt made the following observations about our current interaction with the environment:

---

11   They hunted the Moa to extinction and burnt off much of the forest of the South Island of New Zealand.

12   Cells, which are the building blocks of the human body, replace themselves approximately every eight years, and in nature all things live according to similar cycles of rejuvenation.

1. Society mines and disperses materials faster than they are returned to the Earth's crust (oil, coal, mercury, lead, uranium...)

2. Society produces substances faster than they can be broken down by natural processes—if they can be broken down at all (plastics, building materials, industrial chemicals...).[13]

Karl Henrik Robèrt

3. Society depletes or degrades resources faster than they are regenerated (over-harvesting of trees and fish...) or by other forms of ecosystem manipulation (paving over fertile land, causing soil erosion...)

He concluded that we should aspire to a lifestyle based on cyclic processes compatible with the Earth's natural cycles. This is undeniably logical, and although difficult to implement in our current culture of consumption, it does provide a framework of understanding of what is required.

To achieve such an enlightened and harmonious state of existence, we must develop a culture of custodianship. This is best achieved by emulating some of the ways of traditional cultures such as the Maori, in which land is not owned but cared for by the people who inhabit it. Land ownership is an

---

13   These materials can be prevented from accumulating in the environment if they are managed correctly when they become wastes.

essentially arbitrary legal construct, our planet having existed for 4.5 billion years prior to our short 10,000-year mission to conquer and divide it, and it is sure to exist long after we are gone, boundary pegs, cadastral maps, legal deeds of title and all.

James Lovelock

In his book *Gaia—A New Look at Life on Earth* James Lovelock writes of the marvel that is the fine balance of nature that sustains life on the Earth, where the oceans' salinity levels, temperature, and concentrations of oxygen and carbon dioxide seem almost miraculously to be maintained at the precise levels needed to support life. His key observation is that it is the interconnectedness of life itself—plants and animals interacting with their surrounding environment—that enables this balance to be maintained. To think that we might own the Earth and divide it up to do what we wish, is shortsighted and ignorant and, on a timescale beyond a few generations, foolhardy in the extreme.

To do away with property rights within the bounds of our existing paradigm would seem to be an impossibility, but, at the same time, it is also an imperative. We can see that attempts at tempering the negative environmental effects of capitalism have been mostly futile, and that sentiment is not

The Earth

enough to bring about a system of environmental sustainability. Tough decisions are required, and a cultural shift in attitudes to go along with them. We must deny our wants and needs for the greater ecological good, motivated by the understanding that it is only by reconnecting with the Earth, and by holding it sacred and above all of our material needs, that we may give our children a chance to survive.

The details of how land is to be managed so that production, resource extraction and householding can be maintained obviously still needs to be addressed, but it is clear that stability of tenure would be required. But maverick individualism is not the only context by which this can be achieved. We do not own the Earth, and just as the concept that we may own another person is now relegated to history, regarded now only as a shameful practice based on past ignorance, we must also discard the idea that Nature can be owned and treated as property. It is the Earth that sustains us, and the sacredness of money and property, which is so central to the current religion of materialism, must be replaced by a new reverence for Great Nature.

There should be the capacity for dealing with inherent negativity

Psychologists endlessly debate over nature versus nurture: the extent to which we are externally conditioned or innately predisposed. Were we just born this way, or is it exposure to external stimuli that made us who we are? Without a doubt, both factors are at work. School, work, friends, and the media stimulate us from outside, while our values, reason and faith stimulate us from within.

On a conscious level, we can reason out that it makes sense for us to do things in a certain way, and we are sometimes able to adjust our behavior accordingly. Likewise, when we are emotionally perceptive, we can blend logic with feelings of contextual appropriateness and modify our behavior to fit within the nuances of the situation. We may also be able to draw on our past experiences and knowledge of what works in practice, and apply our common sense. All of these examples suggest that some degree of awareness is operating in our reasoning process.

But more often than not our thinking is not conscious at all, but is essentially an automatic pattern of responses emerging from deeper, unconscious parts of our psyche. Within each of us there is a multitude of diverse influences rooted in our subconscious minds—suggestions that were fed to us as children, conflicting desires, sublimated fears and passions and forgotten traumas and experiences, all percolating up into our decision-making process. Most of our behaviors are reflexive—not really thought through at all—manifestations of patterns of reactions coming from a source of which we remain unaware.

Self-control is of necessity both a conscious and a subconscious process. Although we always try to rationalize our behavior after the fact, not everything that we do is amenable to reason. Subjective factors such as feelings of security, confidence and self-worth can have a big effect on our behavior. The significance of this is obvious to anyone who has brought up a child, and, simple creatures that we are, the same applies to understanding adults.

Thus, to deal with inherently negative behavior, it is essential to create an environment in which it is less likely to manifest. While a small percentage of people has no empathy whatsoever and will thus never make good citizens, the vast majority will respond to an outward code of fairness, if they themselves are treated fairly, by being fair to others. And if people are presented with reasonable living conditions, then they are a lot less likely to revert to destructive behaviors triggered by feelings of frustration, hopelessness or isolation.

An experiment conducted on rats as part of a study on drug addiction in the 1970s illustrated this point.[14] In the first part of the experiment, individual rats were placed in separate cages with nothing but two bowls of water, one laced with co-caine, the other not. In this situation, the rats tended to be-come addicted to cocaine and die. In the second part of the ex-periment the two bowls of water, one also laced with cocaine, were placed in a much larger cage that resembled an environ-ment more natural to a rat, with other rats, a nesting space, a variety of food and an exercise wheel. In this situation, in which the rats were able to live a more fulfilling life, they left the bowl of water laced with cocaine alone.

The second part of a strategy for finding a more enlight-ened way of dealing with inherent negativity is to make justice contextual, a practice commonly called restorative justice. This is an approach to justice that focuses on the needs of the victims and the offenders, as well as those involved in the community, and seeks to produce positive outcomes rather than just dole out punishments.

When we are disconnected from the effects of our nega-tive actions, we are able to get away with a lot more. Not hav-ing to deal with those on the receiving end of our actions makes them easier to justify, or to simply ignore. But when we are forced to meet the consequences of such actions head on, the need for justification becomes acute: either we deny and forsake ourselves, or we confront our actions and feel remorse and shame. Thus, if justice is applied within the context of a community of people who know each other, then much

---

14   The Rat Park Experiment

greater sensitivity and reflexivity becomes possible.[15]

Third, even within an enlightened regime of behavioral regulation, there is still the need to deal with the "bad seeds." And dealt with they must be, for their effect on the whole is insidious and disproportionate to their small number! In some Pacific island cultures, they used to put them in a canoe without a paddle and push them out to sea with enough food for a week, leaving their fate to God. Perhaps such measures are still necessary, although one would hope that there can be found a modern alternative that is more humane.

The uniting principle of this approach to dealing with inherent negativity is that social context is held to be of paramount importance. In any future system, it will be the social context itself that will be the most important factor in managing negative behavior. People must be brought back to prioritizing human relationships above all else—especially de-emphasizing the financial, impersonal legal relationships that provide huge scope for inherently negative behaviors.

If people are connected to each other, and cannot easily escape the effects of their own behavior, then they will be deterred by shame and remorse. Active systems of behavioral control, with explicit boundaries and prescribed punishments, are then only needed to handle rare, extreme cases. But in all other cases behavior is best managed by establishing a social

---

15   The Truth and Reconciliation Commission set up in South Africa at the end of the Apartheid era is noteworthy. Chaired by Nobel Peace Prize winner Archbishop Desomond Tutu, the Commission was mandated to investigate human rights abuses committed by the previous regime. Rather than taking a punitive point of view the Commission worked to restore the dignity of victims and to heal the wounds of the past.

context within which there naturally develop passive systems that reinforce self-control.

A sports team, like any close group working for a common cause, tends to naturally develop a code of behavior in which the team spirit op-

Team spirit

erates as a reconciling force. Some boundaries may still need to be imposed by the coach, but mutual respect, which develops spontaneously in working toward a common aim, tends to be a very effective moderating force.

The more tightly people are connected, and the more able they are to live dignified lives based on stable and respectful relationships, the fewer avenues there remain for unchecked negative behavior to manifest. Provided with the means to make a reasonable life themselves, most people become responsive to the idea of providing a similarly fair deal to those around them.

Democratic principles should be upheld

One system often put forward as an alternative for societal organization is benevolent dictatorship, in which a strong and intelligent leader acts unilaterally to chart a course for the common good. This was the view held by Lee Kwan Yew, who oversaw the establishment of Singapore as a sovereign nation in 1965. He was a believer in strong leadership aligned with good long-term planning and held that the "exuberance of democracy leads to undisciplined and disorderly conditions which are inimical to development." While it is somewhat controversial, there is obviously some merit in his outlook: he was very successful in quickly transforming Singapore from an underdeveloped colonial outpost with few natural resources to a very wealthy country that enjoys relative social harmony.

Lee Kwan Yew

Another testament to the potential effectiveness of benevolent dictatorship is the success of the Ancient Egyptians, who maintained a powerful, strictly authoritarian civilization for 3000 years. They were led by the Pharaoh, who was an absolute monarch, but, unlike numerous more coarse examples of dictatorship, his absolute power was moderated by a well-developed system of religion.[16,17]

---

16   A civilisation that lasted 3000 years must have gone through many permutations, so this is a generalization.

17   The Egyptian religion contained an inner and an outer part, with the general mass of people governed by the external form, based around ritual and a moral code, while the inner part was only known to the select few. Admittance to the inner school was strictly controlled and only the people with the best potential were selected for what was expected to be a life of virtue, inner development and service for the common good. The Pharaoh was part of the inner school of religion. Thus, governance was, in better times, based on more than one man's dictatorial whims.

Temple of Ramses II, Egyptian Pharaoh

But the successes of Lee Kwan Yew and the Ancient Egyptians are exceptional. As we well know, authoritarian rule and dictatorships are fraught with danger. Absolute power is a difficult thing for an individual to handle. The Egyptians, during their better periods, perhaps had an advantage over the Communists in their attempts at maintaining a benevolent dictatorship, because their system was underpinned by spiritual aims, whereas the Communists were devout materialists. But as history would suggest, combining religion with politics also has its dangers—with the potential for particularly virulent and destructive forms of conflict.

Thus, any future system must be democratic, without authoritarian rule.

The system that operates at present in so-called Western liberal democracies doesn't qualify. It is a system rooted in the seventeenth century, back when transportation was by sailboat and by horse and communications by town criers, and it has about as much relevance to the modern day as the powdered wig on a British judge's head. The confines of democratic expression are very narrow and, for most people, it generally amounts to little more than casting a vote every few years to an amorphous entity that they vaguely agree with. Representation and relationships between elected officials and their constituencies are tenuous at best.

British judge wearing a wig

This brings us to the main flaw of modern pseudo-democracy, which is that it centralizes power in the hands self-serving bureaucrats that take decision-making authority away from the people—a sort of institutionalized political corruption. Examples include large corporations, government agencies, ministries and departments, the central banks, the military, and the judiciary. There are also quite a few unelected transnational entities, in the European Union especially, which are able to systematically corrupt the politics of many countries in parallel. In a climate where each special interest group is fighting over its bit of loot, and all are jockeying to cut the electorate out of all decision-making, those who decide to run for public office tend not to have the best interests of the people in mind either. Rather, they tend to be audacious careerists whose main talents are in the areas of moronic insincerity and shallow posturing which the practice of politics requires in this setting.

George Orwell put it well when he said that political language "is designed to make lies sound truthful and murder respectable, and to give an appearance of solidity to pure wind." Luckily, it doesn't really work: the people tend to be smart enough to know that they are being lied to. A somewhat light-hearted 2013 survey completed by Public Policy Polling in the United States found

George Orwell

that the US. Congress had an approval rating of just 9%, while 85% of voters viewed it in a negative light, considering it less popular than cockroaches, head lice, traffic jams, colonoscopies or Genghis Khan.

The problems of society are multidimensional, and so must its politics be if it is to have any hope of solving them. But elected officials are segregated into political parties, which are then arranged along a one-dimensional axis—from left to right. Each party claims some cluster of issues as its own, and plays on the differences between itself and the other parties, concentrating on posturing rather than on substance. Ideally, they succeed in making the act of voting similar to rooting for a certain favorite sports team. It is small wonder, then, that the current system of pseudo-democracy has demonstrably failed in tackling the most significant issues of our time, be they climate disruption, environmental devastation, income and wealth inequality, proliferation of deadly weapons, or the rise of extremist organizations. Moreover, they have made each of these problems much worse!

It is clear that we must try a different approach: in light of all that has already been said here, the new system of democracy must cut out the political professionals who specialize in legalized corruption and instead reconnect people with each other and with their environment.

The Rule of 150

And now we arrive at the rationale for the title of this book. It relates to Dunbar's number: 150, the approximate maximum group size within which people are able to maintain context in their relationships. The reframing of context is the all-important enabler necessary for the establishment of a new reconciling force, which is at the heart of what is necessary for real change. It is a matter of scale: attempts to reconnect people with each other and the environment, and to recontextualize their decision-making, will fail whenever this limit is exceeded.

In applying knowledge of Dunbar's number, we can say that there is a **Rule of 150** that should apply as an organizing principle to the way we structure our systems of human inter-action. We should seek to orient ourselves around what is natural in our evolutionary makeup: we are a social species, we work well as small communities and. Our strength is in working together.

Counter to the emphasis on the collective that follows naturally from the Rule of 150, our current profit-oriented culture promotes the success of the individual, creating a dynamic where the incentive is for people to become silos, set apart in competition, and defined by their individual economic wealth. This creates a vibration of self-protection and insecurity, which fosters isolationism and selfishness, culminating in the cult of the individual that we see celebrated in our modern culture. This situation has brought about much that is degenerate in the modern world.

But there is no need to lament this situation; we can alter it. Built into our DNA is the impulse for something better, based around the welfare and fulfillment of the collective. There is a natural human tendency to want to help others, to create a nurturing environment for our families and safety and security for our communities. Also, in most of us, there is an aspirational impulse for virtue, albeit it is often buried deep and is but a dim flicker.

Maslow's hierarchy of needs provides a theory of human motivation. It defines five broad categories of need, usually shown as a pyramid with the most basic need at the bottom, this being the need for the satisfaction of our physical require-ments for air, food, water, shelter and sleep, while the most as-pirational need of self-actualization, relating to morality, cre-ativity and acceptance, is placed at the very top. In order of importance, these human needs are ranked as follows[18]:

Physiological Needs: These are biological needs. They consist of needs for oxygen, food, water, and a relatively constant body temperature. They are the strongest needs because if a person were deprived of all needs, the physiological ones would come first in the person's search for satisfaction.

Safety Needs: When all physiological needs are satisfied and are no longer controlling thoughts and behaviors, the needs for security can become active. Adults have little awareness of their security needs except in times of emergency or periods of disorganization in the social structure (such as widespread rioting). Children often display the signs of insecurity and the need to be safe.

Needs of Love, Affection and Belongingness: When the needs for safety and for physiological well-being are satisfied, the next class of needs for love, affection and belongingness can emerge. Maslow states that people seek to overcome feelings of loneliness and alienation. This involves both giving and receiving love, affection and the sense of belonging.

Needs for Esteem: When the first three classes of needs are satisfied, the needs for esteem can become dominant. These involve needs for both self-esteem and for the esteem a person gets from others. Humans have a need for a stable, firmly based, high level of self-respect, and respect from others. When these needs are satisfied, the person feels self-confident and valuable as a person in the world. When these needs are frustrated, the person feels inferior, weak, helpless and worthless.

---

18   From *Psychology—The Search for Understanding*

Needs for Self-Actualization: When all of the foregoing needs are satisfied, then and only then are the needs for self-actualization activated. Maslow describes self-actualization as a person's need to be and do that which the person was "born to do." "A musician must make music, an artist must paint, and a poet must write." These

Abraham Maslow

needs make themselves felt in signs of restlessness. The person feels on edge, tense, lacking something, in short, restless. If a person is hungry, unsafe, not loved or accepted, or lacking self-esteem, it is very easy to know what the person is restless about. It is not always clear what a person wants when there is a need for self-actualization.

In order of importance, these human needs are ranked as follows:

1. **Physiological needs**: breathing, food, water, sex, sleep, homeostasis, excretion.
2. **Safety needs**: security of body, of resources, of morality, of the family, of health, of property.
3. **Love and belonging**: friendship, family, sexual intimacy.
4. **Esteem**: self-esteem, confidence, achievement, respect of others.

5. **Self-actualization**: morality, creativity, spontaneity, problem solving, lack of prejudice, acceptance of facts.

The human mind is complex, with many parallel processes happening within it at the same time, and so the satisfaction of one level of need is not necessarily a prerequisite for the fulfillment of another. But it can be loosely said that if the basic needs are met, there is greater potential for energy and effort to be devoted to addressing the others.

The significance of this theory in relation to the Rule of 150 is that belonging to a stable and supportive community provides a context for the attainment of higher aims. Such a context is necessary for us to undertake serious reform of our approach to the environment and to each other.

One of the fundamental weaknesses of the profit motive system is that it is inherently subversive of efforts to provide unconditional security and safety. This weakness manifests to different degrees; even employment in a private enterprise within a market economy can provide a measure security. But, to use the United States as an example, the fact that tens of millions are medicated (and self-medicated) for anxiety and feel the need to protect themselves with apocalyptic levels of weaponry tells us that they have an issue with insecurity. For all the material progress delivered by capitalism, observations of the cultural trends that have accompanied it suggest that there has not been a similar advancement in inner peace or fulfillment.

When people belong to a group bound together by more than mere superficialities, there is a range of mechanisms that are supportive of their human needs. It goes without saying that security must ultimately come from within, and that things such as self-esteem cannot be generated by external circumstances only. But if we understand the importance of providing a stable context in which people can find their footing in life, there is a much greater chance of positive outcomes. Parents looking to create a nurturing environment for their children, for example, are far more likely to succeed when they to have a stable income and roots within a community. Zero-hours contracts, where an employer need not guarantee employees any minimum hours of work or wages, are not consistent with this!

The Rule of 150 also means that groups must be kept small enough to remain functional and effective. When people know each other and interact regularly, there is a constant flow of subtle feedbacks, beyond words, that helps to build the fabric of a shared culture. One knows when one is in harmony with the vibration of the group or not. A verbalized thought resonates, either hanging and falling flat, or comes back amplified through body language and subtly introduced comments. The edges of each individual's radical tendencies are constrained. Through shared experience over time, and knowledge and understanding of the other group members, a true center of gravity is created for the group to reconcile their actions.

When groups operate on this level, the need for an overt democratic process, with activities such as campaigning and voting, is mostly absent. Day-to-day discussion, consensus-based decisions made at spontaneous or scheduled meetings, and a general understanding that all are heading in the same direction, are far superior in generating forward momentum and unity. As has often been said about the process of voting, it is but "two wolves and a lamb deciding who is going to be eaten for lunch."

The process of consensus-based decision-making is gener-ally what occurs in a well-run medium-size business, if it has engaged employees and a positive company culture. Not all have to get along and agree, but because working there im-plies a certain level of performance, or a way of doing things, things generally progress in the right direction. Of course, this requires good management and a stable business environ-ment.

Taking this microcosm of proven effectiveness and apply-ing it to a broader context is not easy. Many of the institutions of modern life require scale. Government, while being respon-sible for much that is broken about our current model, is nec-essary for facilitating such things as the construction and op-eration of water treatment plants, hospitals, schools, roads and public transportation systems. These require large-scale and complex inputs and cannot be executed by a small group in isolation. Scale and specialization are necessary.

The challenge is therefore to address the scourge of large scale, in terms of all the loss of context and nuance that it brings, but to retain the capacity to organize and operate col-lectively to address bigger needs and issues.

This is a tall order!

What we can say as a starting point, though, is that none of the current methods of operating are supportive of the Rule of 150. The trend is toward centralization, depersonalization of the processes of life, and control by rules. The Transpacific Partnership Agreement for example, which is being negotiated at the time of this writing, seeks to elevate the rights of corpo-rations above the level of national law. Transnational businesses are being given a near-untouchable status that will prevent their regulation within a local context, which might otherwise be used to provide some system of ensuring that their activities are appropriate. This can only produce more destruction of the social fabric of society and the concomitant desecration of the environment.

If we are to embark on a journey toward something that can be considered more democratic, in the real sense, where it is not an "us" and "them" system of the leaders and the led, where there is real hope for better outcomes, we must ask ourselves in all situations: "How does this fit in with respect to the Rule of 150?"

Leonard Cohen

This question must become paramount, as decisions must be made by people who maintain relationships with each other and who are engaged in their local context. It is the mechanism by which we may establish a new reconciling force to supplant the profit motive system—a crack through which the light may come in, to borrow a phrase from Leonard Cohen.

Decisions made on a financial basis only, by organizations structured around the management of finance, must be made subordinate to something that is better, more resilient and emerges on its own.

The application of this principle is twofold:

1. On a personal level we can ask ourselves: who are my 150 people?
2. On an organizational level, we can restructure our systems of interaction so that they are based around groups of 150 people.

As individuals, we can reach out to those who form part of our network of belonging, seeking to strengthen the bonds within it. And, as citizens, we can seek to reform our public institutions, making them smaller and more personal. Our inner realm needs to expand, while our outer realm contracts, until the two can meet.

In the first instance, we can all take personal responsibility. Speaking for myself, the first step was in writing this book, and its genesis has been an interesting process. Like most people, I have my identifications in life—work, a young family to support, a household to organize and property to maintain. I live with the feeling of needing to get ahead, to have something in reserve, to progress in my career and to conform to the material expectations dictated by my circumstances. As with many people, the pursuit of these objectives has often come at the expense of relationships, but I have been asking myself, Who are my 150?

The exploration of this question is something that is bound to be personal for each of us, and each of us will have our own angle. Some will find that their 150 is based around their family, others through their vocation, lifestyle or volunteer work. Each person will have a different level of resources to devote to maintaining their networks, but, interestingly, it is usually those who have the fewest possessions who are most

A slum in the Philippines

likely to be able to authentically say that they are in touch
with their 150. Perhaps this is the reason why levels of depression are lower in societies where there is less wealth. From my
time living in the Philippines, where there is much material
want, I was able to compare the psychological state of people
there with those in developed Western countries. Despite the
lack of material resources in the poorer communities, there
was almost always a network of support surrounding each person, and a much lower burden of material expectation. These
networks are much more resilient than one might suppose of a
network of mere friends living independent lives.

In assessing how the Rule of 150 may apply in the great
big world out there, it would be helpful, first of all, if people
were aware of it. This alone would have some positive effect by
prompting them to think hard and attempt to address the

problems of excessive scale. Beyond this, we can only speculate what might be possible.

Prescribing political solutions is rarely the right approach,
and is inherently inferior to defining organizing principles.
But, even though this runs the risk of sounding somewhat
utopian, let us try. Assuming our political systems could be
made to reform themselves to accord with the Rule of 150,
they would be arranged so that groups were kept small enough
for all the participants to be able to represent themselves and
their own interests, and held directly accountable to each
other. To make this work, it would be based on constituencies
of approximately 150 people.

Let us expand a little on the mechanics of such a system,
and clarify some rudimentary details. Within each group of
150 people there is a system of voting that allows leadership
roles (not titles, not positions) to be filled. To organize activities beyond the scale of 150, a hierarchical structure is needed.
To this end, the elected representative of each group would
form a local group with 149 other leaders at a higher level, and
elect a leader to serve one layer up. The representatives would
not form a professional class. However, they would in general
be allowed to serve out terms sufficiently long that they could
get to know each other and form stable working relationships
with those at their level.

In proposing this system, there immediately arises a conflict with the Rule of 150—as soon as we introduce a hierarchy
and the principle of representation. But this is unavoidable.
The aim is to temper, insofar as is possible, the negative effects
of the depersonalization of the political process, and to use
group dynamics as the reconciling force. Whether such dy-

namics could be made to operate in a positive way depends on local culture. For constructive outcomes to be realized, much shared experience and shared need is necessary.

Technology may play a role in making such positive group dynamics achievable in larger groups: There are new modes of interaction evolving, based around social media and communications technology, that are reframing how people can cooperate and collaborate. There is no longer a need for time-intensive face-to-face interaction for people to work together, provided they have issues that they are able to resolve collectively, and provided there is some sort of struggle or formative experience that can serve as the catalyst for bonding.

That which is construed artificially is much more prone to decline and failure, especially if it is based on voluntary participation. But the political process affects people's lives, and hence there is a motive to participate in it. Even if we adopt a completely cynical view of politics, many groups of 150 constituents each could still form a government that could, theoretically, be a force for good.

If this indulgence in abstraction may be excused, a proposed social structure might look as follows:

1. Community: groups of up to 150 people

2. Local Organizing Group: 150 representatives elected by their communities

3. Regional Government: one representative elected by each Local Organizing Group, representing 22,500 people in all

4. National Government: 150 representatives, representing 3,375,000 people each

5. World Council: just 12 people representing 506,250,000 people each

Does this sound far-fetched? Yes, of course! Feel free to poke as many holes in it as you can. Why, it can even be dismissed out of hand as a straw man model of a one-world government fantasist.

But I would argue that it is no more arbitrary than the system we have at present, and, if only as a thought experiment, it is worthy of further consideration. The most obvious refinement is to remove layer number 5 (World Council) from the hierarchy, as that is a sure to be a target of ridicule. In practice, perhaps it would be better if we considered whether such a system could be used to elect officials to serve within the bounds of our existing organizational structures.

In the best case, such a system would be vastly more democratic and provide for much greater accountability. There would be much greater sensitivity to popular will, which would result in more robust decision-making aligned with the needs of ordinary people, rather than the lobbyists, businesses, cronies and self-interested establishment leaders that currently co-opt the political process. The responsiveness of the political process to local nuance would also increase, as would the capacity for people to become more engaged in the management of their local environment.

The formation of alliances along the lines of political parties would still be possible, but as the process of election would be much more personal, ideally there would be no need for candidates for office to be aligned to a party. Instead, elected representatives would be much more likely to be the ones judged to be the best candidates for the job by their peers. The system would tend to promote those with talents for management, and would tend to eliminate greedy, self-serving,

146

power-hungry scoundrels from the process, who would find their decisions challenged by those both above and below them.

Even the highest-ranking officials would be no more than four layers removed from members of their own community, and their ongoing participation in a leadership capacity would be dependent on those 150 people. Any official that loses the support of their own community ceases to be eligible for any higher office. And any official who is seen as favoring his own community to the detriment of others would be unlikely to be chosen to serve one level up. Therefore, this system would be self-limiting when it comes to corruption—which is a curse in our modern world, entrenched at the heart of Wall Street, the City of London and in the halls of governments everywhere.

In such a system, technology would make a tremendous amount of democratic activity possible. It would be straight-forward to call a referendum at any of the four levels of government. The idea that the people could make decisions by referendum on an ongoing, rolling basis is abhorrent to the current political establishment, for an obvious reason: it would make it democratic, rather than the superficial simulation of democracy it currently is!

That is not to say that direct democracy and referendums are a panacea, and the last thing that we would want is an endless debate on the minutiae of all decision-making. What a curse that would be! The extent to which the Swiss make use of referendums in their system would seem to be about the maximum of what is practicable.

What might give such a system added impetus is that the nation-state might fade away—a disconcerting prospect to those who currently hold privileged positions within nation-states. However, in a globalized world, national borders, being largely arbitrary in the first place, are unhelpful in solving problems. For example, much of Africa and the Middle East consists of countries defined by British imperialists and their European contemporaries by drawing lines on maps without any consideration of the huge variety of peoples trapped within these lines. Italy is an agglomeration of what were in the past a constellation of city-states. India is a nation of huge variety with over 100 languages and distinct cultures. China is a nation that is home to 55 ethnic groups including the Muslim Uyghurs, the Buddhist Tibetans, the Han Chinese and nomadic Mongols. Much of the south and west of the United States was recently part of Mexico and is currently being repopulated by Mexicans. Spain and Britain have active separatist movements.

There are many nation-states which are in large part defined by accidents of history and sustained by subjective patriotism. While nationality is central to the identity of many, it can often be transcended by rooting identity in a more local and contextualized level. Thus, in suggesting that the nation state does not have a future, I contend that an alternative system of democracy, as proposed here, would be more support-

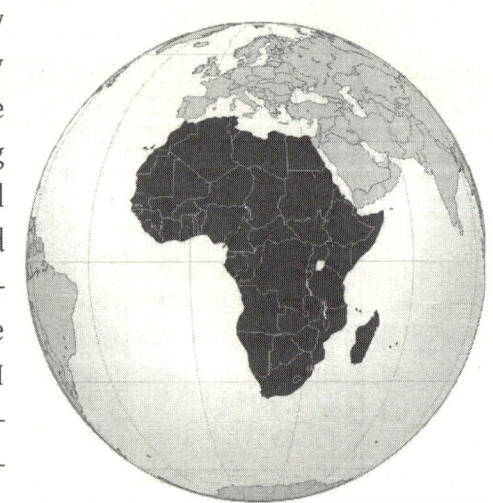

The continent of Africa divided into nation-states

ive of cultural diversity.

In looking to history to provide examples of how previous attempts at similar systems of tiered government might have fared we find that there are no direct comparisons. The Soviet system, from which the Soviet Union took its name, bears some similarities. (A "soviet" is an elected local, district or national council.)

Although the term "soviet" is usually associated with communist states, it was not initially intended to represent only one political force, and a soviet government is essentially

Petrograd Soviet Assembly, 1917

a system of democratic representation. In the Soviet Union the system was set up with workers' and peasants' councils which elected representatives to district, city/province and regional soviets, and so on all the way up to the Supreme Soviet. In its conception it was a system that was a paragon of democracy and it contributed significantly to the early successes of the

Russian experiment with communism.

This interesting account from British journalist H. N. Brailsford, written in 1927, describes how soviets established around factories operated in accordance with the Rule of 150. The passage describes how it was of benefit that the organizing structure was based around groups whose members knew each other through the context of their work.

"The workers in a big factory know each other; they have a common outlook; accustomed to daily association, not merely in work, but in study and recreation, they have a moral unity which the chance inhabitants of a quarter of a great city very rarely achieve. It is no mere metaphor to speak of their common will. It is no less important that they know the records and personalities of the men and women who aspire to represent them, far more intimately than voters in a big democratic

Meeting of the elected management committee
of a Soviet farm, 1935-1940

constituency can usually know the candidates; even when they are local men."[19]

Sadly, such a promising structure of representation never had a chance of enduring success, for there was a much more powerful reconciling force at work. In 1917, in the early days of the Russian Revolution, Lenin had proclaimed that "The workers must demand the immediate establishment of genuine control, to be exercised by the workers themselves." At this time there was already a system of soviet representation in place, and these workers' councils were an established political force.

But the priority of the Bolsheviks, who were a minority political party that Lenin led to power by means of a coup d'état, was not to relinquish control to anyone, be they workers or otherwise. They had

Vladimir Lenin

overthrown a provisional democratic government and were inherently hostile to any form of popular participation in politics that strayed beyond the bounds of their ideology. They employed ruthless methods to suppress real or perceived political enemies, and the small, elite group of Bolshevik revolutionaries which formed the core of the newly established Communist Party dictatorship ruled by decree, enforced by the threat of violence.

19   From: *How the Soviets Work*; H.N. Brailsford, 1927

In the Soviet Union the party elite determined the goals of the state and the means of achieving them in almost complete isolation from the people. They believed that the interests of the individual were to be sacrificed to those of the state, and this was advanced as a sacred social task. Stalin's "revolution from above" sought to build socialism by means of forced collectivization and industrialization, and he oversaw the implementation of programs that entailed tremendous human suffering and loss of life.

By the time the Great Terror of Stalin's reign ended, he had subjected all aspects of Soviet society to strict party-state control, not tolerating even the slightest expression of local initiative, let alone political unorthodoxy. It was a system characterized by strict centralization and disenfranchisement that eventually led to economic decline, inefficiency and apathy. In effect the system that was implemented was a form of state capitalism where the goods and services produced were rendered to the state for the fulfillment of its aims. The more corrupt and repressive the institutions of the state became, the less enthusiastic became the general public in supporting them.

Thus, while a tiered system of government operated in the Soviet Union, its capacity to act as a reconciling force was limited. The operation of group dynamics was constrained within tight boundaries, and in a situation where dissent came at the cost of death or hard labor in Siberia, it was anything but a reflexive, bottom-up system of self-determination. Under the watch of the secret police, the soviets consequently became agencies for the maintenance of unchallenged single-party rule, and little more than dens of corruption where power and influence were divided up among cronies.

What we can deduce from the political arrangements of the Soviet Union, is that they were very successful up to a point, and that the soviet system of tiered government was part of a dynamic that made this success possible. As we discussed in the chapter on Communism, the Soviet Union was a superpower and a world leader for a considerable period of time. This success was not achieved by mere dictatorial directive alone; as tyrannical as their leaders may have been, the ordinary Russian people, like people everywhere, still had lives to live. Space programs, the building out of infrastructure projects and scientific research and advancement do not happen without some amount of spontaneous social engagement. And to this end, the soviet system was constructive.

Therefore, while a system of government based on the Rule of 150, as suggested, might sound fanciful, it is not completely untested. Analysis beyond the brief sketch presented here would be the domain of political scientists, but if nothing less, a case for its further consideration has been made. Our hope for something better rests in creating a context in which a new reconciling force can operate, and the Rule of 150 is a robust principle that can be applied to achieve this goal.

As the Bolsheviks demonstrated, any attempt at change based on one group forcing an ideology upon others is sure to fail. Rather than making a case for change based on any alternative system of economics, or a major redistribution of resources by some agency of authoritarian government, it would be better if we concentrated on creating a new structure for self-organization. If a structure that facilitates the reintroduction of human relationships as primary to the process of decision-making can be implemented, then immediately there will be a change, as a new reconciling force will have been introduced.

It is also a change that is achievable, and being based on political reform oriented around the sole objective of creating a more democratic system, it is something for which a popular, nonradical, nonpartisan mandate could be established.

Work and positive contribution should be incentivized

To this end, the ideal is that selfless service should be the prime motivating force, bureaucracy should be minimized, order should be maintained through group dynamics, land is not to be owned, and government is to be by a system of participatory democracy involving groups of no more than 150 people—all of this supported by information technology that provides transparency, holds people accountable and enables connections and organizational structures to be maintained in a relatively effortless new way that was only made possible recently. Simple! Or barking mad, perhaps.

One refrain we are sure to hear from the doubters is that such notions might be good in theory, but that they just wouldn't work. The first retort is that the current system clearly isn't working, so something else needs to be tried, and very soon! The second is that there is a lot to the proposed alternative that is very practical and common-sense.

Work and struggle are inherent in life and cannot be designed out. Food, shelter, warmth and all those other necessities of society must be provided for. Manufacturing, agriculture, mining and numerous other economic activities must go on, although organized in a different way—without all the waste and vacuous consumption.

The alternate model for production could be extended to factories, farms and distribution networks, could also be organized into groups of 150 people. The Mondragon Cooperative system in Spain provides an excellent case study demonstrating what can be achieved with self-organizing structures. Based on the idea that groups of people acting collectively as equal shareholders in a business can organize themselves into effective business units, an international conglomerate of companies employing over 75,000 people, with an annual revenue in excess of 11 billion Euro, has been created. All this originated from the efforts of just one man, a priest, José María Arizmendiarrieta, motivated to generate work for the young men of his village in the aftermath of the Spanish Civil War.

José María Arizmendiarrieta

This example illustrates that while group dynamics may work best when allowed to develop organically, considerable success can also be achieved by deliberately bringing people together and working according to a well-defined set of organizing principles.

Another organizational theory—one that is complementary to the material already covered—is that of David Snowden, a Welsh management consultant and part-time philosopher. In the course of analyzing management systems, he developed an extreme distaste for rigid systems of rules which, based on ample evidence from his research, result in diminished productivity and creativity, and place limits on innovation. Instead, he proposed that organizations should set clear objectives, establish boundary conditions (basic rules which one shall not transgress for fear of severe punishment), and

David Snowden

then let everyone get to it, amplifying whatever works well and attenuating whatever isn't. This is common sense, you might say, but largely impossible in our current system. This approach allows mistakes to be made, but in our present, somewhat hysterical regime of zero-harm, litigation and political correctness, the woods have been lost for the trees, and rules have replaced discernment, again producing huge waste. The idea that autonomous judgment and initiative should be prioritized over rules requires there to be effective managers capable of making balanced decisions with the support of their subordinates, and that in turn requires trust and loyalty.

Here, we can glimpse something of the dynamic according to which work needs to be restructured. For example, in most modern societies there is a provision for old-age pensions: you pay a part of your income into a fund, and it pays you back upon your retirement. Because the group is huge, such give-and-take is formal and automatic, and happens without scrutiny by the group. Thus we have the untenable situation, in many developed nations, where an ever-shrinking pool of none-too-prosperous working-age people carries the burden of supporting an ever-larger group of rather well-off retirees. In a smaller group, where all inputs and outputs are directly visible to all, there is much less capacity for perpetuating such inequitable arrangements. Once there is an objective set for the entire group to achieve, then, while there will always be a few who are mere passengers, group dynamics will act to motivate most participants to do their part, and team spirit can develop along with the satisfaction of a job well done.

To be sure, the organization of work and the allocation of resources are perennial problems. But a structure that is organized bottom-up, with effective leaders engaged in relationships of reciprocity with those they lead, and with the burden of communication lessened using advanced information systems, surely has the potential for better outcomes than the madness that is our current system, which is so wasteful and perverse that an alternative doesn't even have to be very good in order to be much better. It is also all but assured that the evolution of new technology, which is supplanting labor in the process of production, will increasingly lead to a crisis of employment, which will require work to be addressed in a new way.

8. Action Points

What are you on about?

After finishing the last chapter, I found myself standing at the checkout at my local big box retailer, and it occurred to me just how far removed from our everyday reality all of this seems.

Within the small sample of humanity that surrounded me, there were ordinary people going about their business with absolutely no notion of embarking on a journey toward a new system of organizing our society. There was a young middle-class couple, quite happy with their property rights and their little bit of prosperity, a middle-aged woman with a two-tone hair style and a tattoo of a unicorn on her back, quite clearly knocked about by life, but not a candidate for a discussion about a new system of participatory democracy, and a builder hard at work and keeping his nose clean, who looked like he would just as soon as fly to the moon as commit to a system of broader community engagement.

Yet ultimately this is irrelevant. Like participants in a game of football[20] that is being played on firm sand at low tide, we can carry on the game that is capitalism for a bit longer, but eventually time will be called. Just as King Canute could not stop the tide, neither can we stop the forces that are steadily building toward the inevitable unraveling of the profit motive-driven system. At that point there will be no choice but to start doing things differently.

Change

On the nature of change, systems theorist John G. Bennett described the process as thus:

"Change is in the nature of harvest, the seeds of which have first to be sown, then go through the whole process of lying for a time within the ground, of germinating, of appearing above the earth and finally in its own season giving the harvest."

In the flux that is being created by the various disturbances to our status quo there is fertile ground for the germination of something new, and to this end there are ideas whose time may have come.

Nothing comes from wishful thinking, and transformation can only come through struggle and sacrifice. In the Hindu tradition, the goddess Kali is worshiped as the purveyor of destruction, but also venerated as a giver of life, since it is from destruction that new beginnings can be created. It is death which makes room for new life to spring forth.

20 Known as "soccer" in the US.

160

The drivers that underpin the struggle for change must also be strong, or whenever there are setbacks, or obstacles to overcome, impetus will be lost. Often the imperative of survival provides the impetus for change, and maybe it is necessary that we be truly imperiled and stripped of our way of life for there to be sufficient galvanization of purpose to start doing things differently. Refugees fleeing from

Hindu goddess Kali

their homes in a time of war or famine have no choice but to confront their changing situation with vigor if they wish to survive, and maybe this is the situation that we will be presented with.

One scenario painted by the Zeitgeist Movement is that it is possible for a new technology-based system to replace the capitalist system. Such a system would be based on decentralization and democracy and the free production of goods and services for all. In a recent interview, Zeitgeist founder Peter Joseph spoke of many of the themes raised in this book, and explained his vision for an alternative future much along the lines of what has been described here. Specifically, his idea is that public finances could be used to build an infrastructure where the basic needs of society are provided free of charge for all using automated systems, and that a transition period from our existing scarcity-based market economy to an abundance-based "natural law" economy could be facilitated by paying a state-funded basic living wage to all.

But Joseph's proposal seems to be missing a key element.

Peter Joseph

There is no doubt that technological change is reshaping our society and will continue to do so at an accelerating pace. Yet it seems that the core issue to be addressed is altogether more human, and an overreach in our faith in technology is, in part, what has brought us to this point in the first place. After all, it has been easy to produce enough food to feed all the people in the world for a long time, yet hunger still persists, leading one to question whether there is a darker side to humanity that needs to be addressed.

Sebastião Salgado, Brazilian photographer and the subject of the film *The Salt of the Earth*, has made it his life's work to capture the essence of the human condition, a pursuit which has brought him international acclaim, but which almost drove him to a point of despair beyond all hope.

In describing his inner calling as a photographer, Salgado relates how he felt compelled to document the stories of ordinary people and their struggles in life. This urge led him to

162

serve as a witness to mass starvation during the famines of Central Africa in the mid 1980s, and the horror of ethnic cleansing in the civil war in Yugoslavia in the early 1990s. During the genocide that enveloped Rwanda in 1994 he acted as an indomitable documenter of truth, journeying into the country along a road along which a terrified multitude was fleeing,

Sebastião Salgado

passing the corpses of tens of thousands who had been recently murdered. He spent many months there and witnessed the absolute worst of humanity, misery upon misery, as desperate, starving people received no mercy whatsoever, and death stalked everyone around him. In Salgado's own words:

"When I left there I no longer believed in anything, any salvation for the human species. You couldn't survive such a thing. We didn't deserve to live. No one deserved to live. How many times did I lay my cameras down to cry over what I had seen?"

And, as his biographers described in The Salt of the Earth:

"Sebastião had seen into the heart of darkness, and deeply questioned his work as a social photographer and a witness of the human condition. What was left for him to do after Rwanda?"

Skulls at a Rwandan genocide memorial site

Salgado's account encapsulates the challenges we face. Our human attachments are very strong, to the point where many may choose to die, or to kill many others, to hold onto them. And it is unrealistic to think that the attitudes that have become entrenched around our profit motive-driven system could easily be relinquished.

Yet, in a remarkable twist, in the story of Sebastião hope was also rekindled, which also serves as a source of hope for us all. His father had been a rancher, farming land cleared of rainforest. It was initially productive, but quickly became arid, afflicted by drought and degradation of soil quality. After his time in Rwanda. Salgado returned to this barren land, and his wife Lelia, seeking to lift the spirits of the family, came up with the idea of replanting the rainforest—a journey she related as follows:

"I remember during the first plantation, I sometimes dreamt that everything had died. Because the soil was so bad here. So damaged. I asked myself "will it ever grow?" The *Mata Atlantica* [Atlantic Rainforest] has 400 species. Of course we don't have all 400 of them, but each time we plant, it is 100 species, 150 species. After the first planting 60% died, after the second 40%. We had no book to tell us how to replant the *Mata Atlantica.*"

Mata Atlantica

As a result of their determination the Salgados were extremely successful in reforesting the family ranch, and they formed an institute, the Instituto Terra, to expand their efforts throughout the valley where they lived. Over 4 million trees have now been planted and the life of the land has returned to this small area of a once great rainforest. The hills have become lush once again, and, in parallel with this rebirth, Sebastião's hope for humanity has also returned. In his despair he had taken to tending to the Earth, and in doing so he found a new perspective on life. After years documenting suffering, he decided to embark on an altogether different mission: to photograph the unspoiled corners and cultures of the world, of which he discerned there were still many.

Perhaps Salgado's example offers a way forward for the world.

The viral nature of change

Interestingly, societal change is usually led by a small minority who influence the view of the majority. Noam Chomsky describes this process as "manufacturing consent," where control of information channels is used to consciously direct the development of our cultural narratives. In its grossest manifestation, this involves the dissemination of deliberately biased and sometimes outright false propaganda by those who have vested interests and power. Chomsky cites the example of how Woodrow Wilson won the presidency of the United States in 1916 having run on a platform of peace that reflected the citizenry's very strong objection to being drawn into World War I. In fact, Wilson had no such convictions and, once elected, he

Noam Chomsky

quickly set about putting the United States on a course toward war.

Wilson established a state propaganda agency called the Committee of Public Information, which, in Chomsky's words, was provided with a brief to "propagandize the population into a jingoist hysteria." At this they were extremely successful. In Chomsky's words: "within a few months there was a raving war hysteria and the US was able to go to war." This made a big impression on a young soldier by the name of Adolf Hitler, who was able to put this lesson in the power of propaganda to his own nefarious use at a later date. National security and intelligence agencies employ the same template today.

In describing the effectiveness of propaganda as a tool for the minority to shape the opinions of the majority, we can observe an interesting corollary. Yes, people with hidden agendas use deliberately seeded stories and narratives to direct public opinion. But ordinary stories and narratives that resonate with people can quite spontaneously have the same effect. In the lead-up to the Arab Spring, the catalyst was the story of a 26-year-old Tunisian man, Mohamed Bouazizi —an ordinary citizen

Woodrow Wilson

and the breadwinner for his widowed mother and six siblings, who was victimized by the police in his home town for not having a permit to sell fruits and vegetables at the market. When the police asked Bouazizi to hand over his wooden

Mohammed Bouazizi

cart, he refused. Then, a policewoman allegedly slapped him. Deeply angered, publicly humiliated and deprived of his means of supporting his family, Bouazizi marched in front of a government building and set himself on fire. This act of desperation immediately resonated with others in the town, who then began protesting. These protests were filmed using cell phone cameras and shared on the Internet, catalyzing further protest. Within days protests started popping up across the country, calling upon the Tunisian President and his government to step down. A little over a month later the president fled and his regime collapsed.

The fact that this spontaneous upwelling of public sentiment quickly descended into something quite malicious is the subject of a different story. The uprisings that ensued across North Africa and the Middle East were buoyed by a popular wish for change, backed up by people with a deep need, to the extent that they were prepared to sacrifice everything. But for all their efforts, without any better structure or vision to organize themselves around, positive change has been hard to discern. The lot of the citizens of the countries caught up in the

Arab Spring movement has generally devolved into something worse than what they had, and in the case of Syria, Libya and Yemen, civil war reigns. Also of note is that while the quest for democracy that underpinned the Arab Spring movement was perceived as a virtuous cause by most, it also opened a convenient back door for others with different agendas to achieve more dubious geopolitical objectives. There is well-founded speculation, for example, that the conflict in Syria has as much to do with instigating a regime change so that a gas pipeline can be built from the Middle East to Europe, as it does with democratic reform.

While the unfolding of the Arab Spring illustrates how media channels inevitably attempt to reframe stories such as that of Mohamed Bouazizi to accord with their own biases, there is a human aspect to them that defies attempts at misappropriation. News that touches people on an empathetic level can cast issues in a new light and have a huge effect in shaping cultural consensus. Given an appropriate set of circumstances, momentous change has something of a chaotic quality, where small events can trigger significant shifts.

This is a theme explored in Malcolm Gladwell's book *The Tipping Point: How Little Things Can Make a Big Difference*, which illustrates how cultural shifts evolve from small beginnings. Gladwell describes how "Ideas

Malcolm Gladwell

and products and messages and

behaviors spread like viruses do" and he defines a cultural tipping point as "the moment of critical mass, the threshold, the boiling point" where a fringe idea or fad crosses over into a mass phenomenon. As an example, Gladwell describes how in a surprisingly short period of time New York was transformed from being an incredibly dangerous, crime-infested city in the 1980s into a relatively safe, law-abiding city—achieved through such seemingly minor initiatives as painting over graffiti, fixing broken windows and tackling petty crimes and misdemeanors such as jaywalking. It is acknowledged that, in the usual swing of the pendulum associated with such attempts at radical change, the police in many instances have overstepped reasonable boundaries in achieving this objective. For example, part of the strategy to improve safety in New York was to implement a stop-and-frisk system, where police officers could search citizens at their discretion.[21]

Dipping into the world of collapse theorists

A lively community of collapse theorists exists online, who are informed by such seminal texts as Joseph Tainter's *Collapse of Complex Societies* and Jared Diamond's *Collapse*, and who are waiting, almost eagerly, for the demise of our civilization, looking out for signs of its approaching end. Among them is Dmitry Orlov, a Russian-born original thinker, who first came to notice through his comparison of the collapse of the Soviet

---

21   In 2002 police records show a total of 97,296 stop-and-frisk searches were completed, but by 2011 this figure had risen to 685,724. The system is particularly resented by the city's Black and Latino communities, who legitimately suggest that it amounts to systematic intimidation and harassment.

Union with what he sees to be the similar and unfolding collapse of the United States. In his thought-provoking book, *The Five Stages of Collapse*, Orlov delineates a taxonomy of collapse. Orlov ties each of the five stages of collapse to the breaching of a specific level of trust in relation to the status quo.[22]

Stage 1: Financial collapse. Faith in "business as usual" is lost.

Stage 2: Commercial collapse. Faith that "the market shall provide" is lost.

Stage 3: Political collapse. Faith that "the government will take care of you" is lost.

Stage 4: Social collapse. Faith that "your people will take care of you" is lost.

Stage 5: Cultural collapse. Faith in "the goodness of humanity" is lost.

Reflecting upon the relevance of this taxonomy to the current situation, it becomes clear that we are close to a breach of trust on some levels. In 2008 we saw a near-collapse of the financial system, when Lehman Brothers declared bankruptcy, triggering a cascading series of defaults that threatened to bankrupt numerous banks around the world. The problems that caused it have not been solved—nor, it would ap-

Dmitry Orlov

22   More recently he has also proposed a sixth stage of collapse, which is a collapse of the environment that sustains us.

pear, can they ever be solved.

At the time of this writing, Greece has been on the cusp of financial collapse for some time. Some degree of commercial and political collapse has clearly occurred there, with economic activity contracting 25% since the onset of the global financial crisis. Trust in government has diminished to such an extent that many people have stopped paying their taxes. Greece's outright financial collapse has been delayed by its Eurozone membership: European Union officials have kept bailing it out, largely to protect the banks in their home countries. But, for all their efforts in forestalling the inevitable, Greece's slide into a national state of dysfunction continues apace, and all nations of the European Union face a similar fate in due course.

Thus we see that Orlov's taxonomy provides a relevant context, in which we can conceptualize how any future system-wide shocks might unfold, potentially cascading from financial, to commercial, and then on to political and social collapse. Orlov isn't alone in thinking along these lines: the former Greek finance minister Yanis Varoufakis has admitted that when he first considered the prospect of a Greek or European-wide financial

Yanis Varoufakis

172

collapse, part of him welcomed the prospect of such failure, because as a socialist he hoped that something new and better could be put into place. But he said that he changed his mind once he thought things through: working out how such a collapse would play out made him realize that it would be catastrophic for the Greek people, and that it was far better to try and hold things together for the time being, buying some time for something better to be worked out.

As Orlov is quick to point out, collapse is a faulty product: "unsafe at any speed and impossible to sell." People prefer to bury their heads in the sand than accept the reality of imminent collapse, for it implies that the pretense for a whole range of established life activities—such as caring about accumulating money—is invalid. The ready retort of the deniers is that the end of the world has been foretold many times before; we still have lives to live, and what is the use of being a "prepper" or "doomer"?

The prescription to this situation provided by another prominent collapse theoretician, John Michael Greer, is to "collapse now and avoid the rush." Greer advocates "voluntary simplicity", suggesting that we bypass irreconcilable global economic problems and embrace a fulfilling alternative life-

John Michael Greer

style, which, in and of itself, offers a lot more than the present high-stress, time-poor, relationships-"lite" mode of living.

There is a poster that many will have seen on the internet which states the following:

"When asked what surprised him about humanity the most, the Dalai Lama replied:

'Man surprised me most about humanity. Because he sacrifices his health in order to make money. Then he sacrifices money to recuperate his health. And then he is so anxious about the future that he does not enjoy the present; the result being that he does not live in the present or the future; he lives as if he is never going to die; and then dies having never really lived.'"

To this end, it would seem that Greer has a point. (Like many quotes distributed on the Internet, the source of the quote is false—the Dalai Lama did not say these words.)

This changes everything

One of the greatest threats facing humankind is catastrophic, runaway climate change, triggered by long-term changes to the composition of Earth's atmosphere caused by the burning of fossil fuels. Scientific debate is over on a large set of predictions: a greater than 2ºC global average temperature rise is guaranteed[23]; most coastal cities will be lost as ocean levels rise; the loss of glaciers will cause widespread drought and starvation as the fertile plains beneath them dry out; extreme weather events will increase in frequency and power, causing ever-greater destruction. Continuing research attempts to

---

23 Barring a large asteroid impact, catastrophic volcanic eruption or some other unlikely but possible climate-disrupting cataclysm.

quantify what will happen and when, and how bad it could get. Preliminary answers range from decades to centuries, and from harsh but survivable conditions to near-term human extinction. At the same time, actual observations show that the rate of climate change is far outpacing most predictions.

James Hansen

Dire predictions are now mainstream. Two generations of people who have grown up aware of the severity of the environmental issues we face, and the idea that little can be done to address these issues within the confines of the profit motive-driven system is starting to catch on. Leading US climate-change scientist James Hansen and a team of sixteen leading climate scientists recently issued a dire warning that inaction means the Earth is now entering a Hyper-Anthropocene age, with sea-level rise on an exponential growth rate that could result in a 10-foot (3.048 meter) sea level rise sooner rather than later. In a conclusion that is somewhat beside the point, Hansen and his colleagues predict that the economic cost will be "practically incalculable."

In capturing something of the shift in outlook that the specter of climate change is bringing about among the general population, Naomi Klein has concluded that neither green eco-

nomics, nor the benevo-
lent efforts of sympa-
thetic billionaires, nor
the rollout of interna-
tional treaties and con-
ventions are of much
use at all in tackling the
issue at hand. She fur-
ther asserts that this is
because they go against
the fundamental nature
of our current system,
which is focused on

John Lennon

growth and consumption. Somewhat radically, but completely
in accordance with the message of this book, she also con-
cludes that we must reexamine the role of capitalism in our society, for, to quote Klein: "our economic model is at war with
life on Earth." Indeed, we must!

You say you want a revolution

As John Lennon sang, "you say you want a revolution", and
"we'd all love to see the plan." This seems like a sensible idea.
The world has seen plenty of radical firebrands, and the results
they have produced have been almost uniformly ghastly. If
there is to be a way forward, it had better be through peace.
There is no value in swinging between pairs of opposites, and
what can serve to unite people to face the challenges that
await us is what is of most value.

There is also some merit in adopting the view of the former Greek finance minister, Yanis Varoufakis: that we must

seek to hold together the fabric of our current system, while at the same time working to identify and implement alternative social, economic and political models that might help us confront the challenges we face. Indeed, if we consider Dmitry Orlov's taxonomy of collapse, it is easy to see that there is no merit in further destabilizing the current system unless we can put something better in its place. Financial collapse is entirely possible in the foreseeable future, as it has been since 2007, and the prospect of this leading to commercial collapse or political collapse is not enticing. But the prospect of such cascading failure is very real: the current political system is enmeshed with the financial world, and it is easy to see how public disorder might ensue if there were any sudden shock that challenged the general public's faith in the current system of money. Perhaps in preparation for just such an event, governments are proceeding to shore up the centralization of political power through the militarization of police, passing laws with repressive and totalitarian undertones, and establishing mass surveillance systems.

A far better approach is to work on decoupling finance, commerce and politics, so that if the financial and commercial world did become destabilized, there would be some organizational infrastructure left standing. It would allow order to be kept through decentralized, local systems of

Los Angeles Police Department SWAT officer

governance, which would avoid a lot of the unnecessary and ultimately self-defeating use of force.

Where do we go from here?

In light of the material presented here so far, here is a short list of constructive action points that might serve to provide a pathway forward:

1. Educate yourself and others about the insidious nature of the profit motive in its capacity as the reconciling force of our society.

2. Commit to the idea that nothing but the replacement of the profit motive as our societal reconciling force will ever bring about effective change.

3. Seek to observe the workings of the Rule of 150 in your own life—to work out who your 150 are and strengthen your bonds with them, so that you may come to know the power of service to a group as a positive reconciling force.

4. Reject our current system of democracy and agitate for a reformation of our political arrangements around a bottom-up, information systems approach with constituencies of no more than 150 people.

5. Fight attempts by establishment media and government organizations to entrap people in war and conflict.

6. Embrace the rollout of new technology as an agent of economic and environmental transformation.

7. Don't underestimate the power of unified thought to effect change.

8. Embrace the philosophy that small efforts widely disseminated can have a cumulative positive effect much greater than the sum of its parts. (Look for cultural "tipping points" to

breach, then build momentum.)

9. Enjoy the process. Remember that by working toward becoming strong, balanced and capable of independent thought and understanding, we can have a profound effect on our surrounding environment.

Once something is observed and understood, that understanding can create inner tension and moral obligation. In the world of health and safety there is a rule that if you see a problem and you walk past it, it becomes your problem. The same principle should apply in all areas of our lives. And so, once we have understood that the profit motive is the problem, that it cannot be fixed, and that it is causing us great harm, it becomes difficult to continue to accept our way of life as it is. There is a moral imperative to at least be open to alternatives. In the course of exploring these alternatives, our thoughts have the potential to align, and become imbued with a new collective power.

Katniss Everdeen, The Hunger Games

There is clearly a reservoir of latent energy, expectant of change, waiting to be directed. Just look at the success of the many recent big budget films on dystopian themes—such as The *Hunger Games*, *Interstellar*, *Mad Max*, *Elysium* and *The Road*. These films are thought-provoking, causing more people to question where our current path is leading us. They also allow us to reflect—expressing a trepidation about a future that we know already exists. Even among those who are not politically engaged there seems to be a consensus building—that if things carry on the way they are, the outcomes will not be particularly good.

Wrapping up

This book puts forth the idea that the Rule of 150 may be an antidote to the ills of the profit motive system. The central idea is that service to a group of connected people, bonded by a common cause, is a viable and powerful alternative to the profit motive. This is a conjecture supported by research into our evolutionary biology and the historical record of humankind. The present elevation of the status of the individual is an aberration, in conflict with the natural state of the human species, who are inherently cooperative and sociable.

Capitalism has been one of the major drivers in the evolution of modernity, and, as it has become ever more central to our way of life, historical arrangements of community have been eroded and the challenges of scale increased. Our hope is that we may redress this imbalance, finding strength in relationships and eliminating the impersonal structures that are the cause of so many of our problems. An essential part of this process is to establish a new context for decision making and resource distribution.

It is impossible to say whether anything meaningful might be achievable on a large scale. Addressing global problems is treacherous territory: it is hard to speak about "global interest" without sounding foolhardy. What we can say, with absolute certainty, is that the Rule of 150 is a thoroughly useful principle to apply to one's own life, and worthy of further reflection.

In applying the Rule of 150 we must take an approach that is rather different to what is currently considered normal. Specifically it makes it necessary to decompartmentalize our relationships. One of the chief failings of our current arrangement is that it allows us to be anonymous, and to limit the extent to which we allow our relationships to become personal.

Large-scale systems of interaction make it possible for relationships to be transient. If we are not intimately connected with those with whom we have dealings, we can manage the extent to which we are considerate toward them. If we need to do something that goes against the grain of a relationship, the damage that is caused may be tolerable, and in situations where we may need to forsake the interests of another to protect our own, we can make a calculated decision that we have no choice but to act in a selfish way. In keeping with the vibration of our "throwaway society" we might never have to see those on the receiving end again, the relationship being essentially expendable.

Adherence to the Rule of 150 means that our dealings with each other must be personal, in the context of a lifelong association. Thus, there must always be found a resolution to any conflict that is considerate of the other parties involved. It is the nature of lifelong personal relationships that they cannot be severed without causing extensive damage.

For example, the butcher in a village who lives next door to his customers is unlikely to sell them bad meat. If a young child that he knew were to become ill and permanently disabled due to e. coli poisoning from meat supplied by him, then this would make life very uneasy for him. But in a situation where meat is processed in a large slaughterhouse and distributed through supermarkets or fast food chains there is very little contact between the suppliers and their customers. Decisions around food safety are made by technicians and bureaucrats who have little contact with the end-users of their products. They can compartmentalize their relationships with those eating their meat, leaving it up to public health officials, insurance companies and corporate lawyers if something goes wrong.

In more extreme cases, the compartmentalization of relationships may allow someone to be a monster at work, say, criminalizing mental illness and placing psychotic or demented patients in solitary confinement, but a gentle, loving husband and parent at home. But if you only deal with the 150 people who all know each other, such disconnects become impossible.

The Rule of 150 demands that we develop a functioning, harmonious relationship with 150 people, and this obviously presupposes being considerate toward them. Naturally, there will always be minor ongoing conflicts, but in the context of a group of people bound by the Rule of 150 this is done with the realization that between n people who all know each other there are $n(n-1)/2$ relationships to be sustained, which, for a single group of 150 people, gives us 11,175 relationships. In this situation power is not one-sided, and even when disagreements occur, in all but the most extreme cases the door must be kept open for compromise and resolution. In this situation, solutions cannot be dictated by rules or the threat of punishment, and there must always be the capacity for discernment of nuance and the accommodation of specific circumstances.

Often we hear it said that we should not go into business with friends, the idea being that business sometimes requires one to be hard-nosed and businesslike, and that's not how one conducts a relationship with friends. But the Rule of 150 not only requires doing business with friends, it means that one needs to sustain that relationship in a friendly fashion. It requires us to transform the nature of friendship and the nature of work to make the two compatible.

The implication of the Rule of 150 is that it is impossible to walk away from people—to part on bad terms—so messy break-ups become unlikely. Instead, everyone makes an effort to patch things up rather than risk allowing relationships to cool and descend into a spiral of alienation and hostility. Unconditional acceptance by a group of 150 people also means that a positive and supportive psychological context is generated by membership in the group, creating a platform of stability and support. Mental illness, which often develops as a result of individuals becoming alienated and depressed, has much less of an opportunity to take hold.

Lastly, when 150 people take responsibility for one another, they gain an incredible amount of power—actual power, because each of them becomes willing to make a serious sacrifice for the sake of the group, knowing that each person in the group will do the same.

Expand your horizons

Our present capitalist system is essentially governed by an unsustainable set of materialistic rules which are primarily concerned with the efficient flow of commerce and the management and distribution of things. The solution proposed is to

The Buddha

turn that emphasis on its head, so that social and environmental needs are given priority. That we may engage with each other according to a system that is dynamic, where the human values of solidarity, empathy and respect for each other might flourish, rather than being stifled by a system that is mechanical and insentient in nature. Organization around the principle of the Rule of 150 is an approach that is elegant in its simplicity and provides the scope for change to develop according to its own course.

Living in a materialist culture, we have been conditioned to believe that matter is all there is, but this is a conclusion based on abductive reasoning[24], and is therefore only a state-

---

24   Abductive reasoning is a form of logical inference that goes from an observation to a hypothesis that accounts for the observation, seeking to find the simplest and most likely explanation. For example, our medieval ancestors determined that the stars were pinpricks of light emanating from

ment of opinion. There is much that is subtle, that we cannot yet perceive of or conceive of within the prism of our five senses, which science cannot adequately observe or measure—particularly when it comes to our relationships with each other and our interaction with the world around us.

In seeking to extricate ourselves from the torpor of our current situation, let us hope that we may be able to see each other in a new light—as sensitive beings worthy of respect and consideration—and that by so doing we may come under the influence of a force that suffuses the Cosmos, which the Buddha described as Divine Compassion.

---

the heavens, this being the most logical explanation according to a process of abductive reason, and the idea that a single pinprick of light could in fact be billions of stars within a galaxy would have been dismissed.

Photo Credits

100 Trillion Zimbabwe dollars: by Reserve Bank of Zimbabwe - Licensed under Public Domain via Commons.

1920s milking technology: Shutterstock id 2367319.

Abraham Maslow: Via Wikipedia. Licensed under Public Domain via Commons.

Adam Smith: by Unknown. Licensed under Public Domain via Commons.

Albatross Chick Midway Island: Permission received by email from Jordan Studios on 24/12/15 to use 1 greyscale image.

Albert Einstein: by Orren Jack Turner, Princeton, N.J. Licensed under Public Domain via Commons.

Aldous Huxley: by Not given. Licensed under Public Domain via Commons.

Andrei Kurkov: Via Wikipedia. Licensed under Public Domain via Commons.

Antilia Building Mumbai: "Ambani house mumbai" by Jhariani . Licensed under CC BY-SA 3.0 via Commons.

Aristotle: by Copy of Lysippus - Jastrow (2006). Licensed under Public Domain via Commons.

Ayn Rand: Via Wikipedia. Licensed under Public Domain via Commons.

British judge wearing wig: Via Wikipedia. Licensed under Public Domain via Commons.

Charles Darwin: Via Wikipedia. Licensed under Public Domain via Commons.

Charles Dickens: by Jeremiah Gurney - Heritage Auction Gallery. Licensed under Public Domain via Commons.

Charlie Munger: Kent Sievers / Shutterstock.com.

Communist Collective Farm: Shutterstock id 339962990.

Cyril Parkinson: Via Wikipedia. Licensed under Public Domain via Commons.

David Snowden: Via Wikipedia. Licensed under Public Domain via Commons.

Dead fish floated in dark water: Shutterstock id 293104013.

Dmitry Orlov: by Natasha Orlov, used by permission.

Eric Garner: Shutterstock id 206914753.

Ford Factory 1913: Via Wikipedia. Licensed under Public Domain via Commons.

Ford Factory 2014: Shutterstock id 279735305.

George Orwell: Via Wikipedia. Licensed under Public Domain via Commons.

Hank Paulson: "Henry Paulson official Treasury photo, 2006" by Treasury Department. Licensed under Public Domain via Commons.

Haruhiko Kuroda: by Asian Development Bank. Licensed under CC BY 2.0 via Commons.

Homesteaders: by Unknown. Licensed under Public Domain via Commons.

Indian Goddess Kali: Via Wikipedia. Licensed under Public Domain via Commons.

Indian Tipi Camp: by W. H. Jackson. Licensed under Public Domain via Commons.

James Hansen: Via Wikipedia. Licensed under Public Domain via Commons.

Jeremy Rifkin: Via Wikipedia. Licensed under Public Domain via Commons.

John Lennon: Via Wikipedia. Licensed under Public Domain via Commons.

John Michael Greer: Via Wikipedia. Licensed under Public Domain via Commons.

John Steinbeck: Via Wikipedia. Licensed under Public Domain via Commons.

José María Arizmendiarrieta: Via Wikipedia. Licensed under Public Domain via Commons.

Joseph Stalin: Via Wikipedia. Licensed under Public Domain via Commons.

Karl Henrik Robèrt: Flickr.

Karl Marx: by original unknown. Licensed under Public Domain via Commons.

Katniss Everdeen: Via Wikipedia. Licensed under Public Domain via Commons.

Kim Il Sung: Via Wikipedia. Licensed under Public Domain via Commons.

LAPD SWAT Officer: Flickr.

Lee Kwan Yew: Flickr.

Leonard Cohen: Via Wikipedia. Licensed under Public Domain via Commons.

Lord Acton: Via Wikipedia. Licensed under Public Domain via Commons.

Mahatma Gandhi: by No 9 Army Film & Photographic Unit. Licensed under Public Domain via Commons.

Malcolm Gladwell: by PEN American Center - Philip Kerr and Malcolm Gladwell. Licensed under CC BY 2.0 via Commons.

Manila Slum: Via Flickr.

Mao Zedong: Via Wikipedia. Licensed under Public Domain via Commons.

Matapo, a blind tohunga: Via Wikipedia. Licensed under Public Domain via Commons.

Meeting of the elected management committee of a Soviet farm 1935-1940: Shutterstock id 339956744.

Mohamed Bouazizi: Via Wikipedia. Licensed under Public Domain via Commons.

Naomi Klein: by Joe Mabel. Licensed under CC BY-SA 3.0.

Newton's Third Law: by Benjamin Crowell. Licensed under CC BY-SA 3.0 via Commons.

Noam Chomsky: by Duncan Rawlinson, from Flickr. Licensed under CC BY 2.0 via Commons.

Nuremberg Rally 1936: Shutterstock id 251930365.

Oscar Wilde: Via Wikipedia. Licensed under Public Domain via Commons.

Peter Joseph: Permission to use image as per email from copyright holder Nikola Danaylov dated 6 Jan 2016.

Peter Kropotkin: by F. Nadar - NYPL. Licensed under Public Domain via Commons.

Petrograd Soviet, 1917: Via Wikipedia. Licensed under Public Domain via Commons.

Pol Pot: Via Wikipedia. Licensed under Public Domain via Commons.

Political Map of Africa: Via Wikipedia. Licensed under Public Domain via Commons.

Pope Francis: "Canonization 2014"- Licensed under CC BY-SA 2.0 via Commons.

Robin Dunbar: Via Wikipedia. Licensed under Public Domain via Commons.

Rocky IV: Via Wikipedia. Licensed under Public Domain via Commons.

Russell Brand: Fair use; screen grab from "The Trews" show.

San Bushmen, Namibia: Shutterstock id 167527046 .

Scales of Justice, London Criminal Court: Shutterstock id 26325739.

Sebastiao Salgado: Via Wikipedia. Licensed under Public Domain via Commons.

Starvation: Via Wikipedia. Licensed under Public Domain via Commons.

Steve Jobs: by Matthew Yohe - Own workLicensed under CC BY 3.0 via Commons.

Structure of Atom: Shutterstock Image 143915434; Copyright snapgalleria.

Supermarket Meat Counter: Shutterstock id 217895515 .

Sword of Damocles: Via Wikipedia. Licensed under Public Domain via Commons.

Tao: Shutterstock image: 230605423; Copyright researcher97.

Team Spirit: Shutterstock id 73284739.

Temple of Ramses II: Shutterstock id 67057171.

The Buddha: Shutterstock id 184571084.

The Earth: Via Wikipedia. Licensed under Public Domain via Commons.

The Mata Atlantica: Via Wikipedia. Licensed under Public Domain via Commons.

The Sun: "Sunspots and Solar Flares" by NASA. Licensed under Public Domain via Commons.

Thomas Paine: Via Wikipedia. Licensed under Public Domain via Commons.

Trident Submarine: Flickr /defenceimages/8950656444.

Two Wolves: Shutterstock id 117359659.

Vivekananda: by Unknown. Licensed under Public Domain via Commons.

Vladimir Lenin: Shutterstock id 339956711.

Winston Churchill: by United Nations Information Office, New York - Library of Congress, Reproduction number LC-USW33-019093, digital ID fsa.8e00870. Licensed under Public Domain via Commons.

Woodrow Wilson: Via Wikipedia. Licensed under Public Domain via Commons.

Yanis Varoufakis: Via Wikipedia. Licensed under Public Domain via Commons.

Index

honesty: 84
hope: 24-5, 31-2, 50, 74, 84, 98, 109, 141, 153, 164-5, 173, 180, 185
hopelessness: 126
horse-drawn buggy: 87
horse: 132
hospitals: 107, 140
hostile environments: 118
hostility: 183
household items: 94
housing: 63
human:
    condition: 162-3
    contact: 25
    fallibility: 113
    misjudgment: 7
    nature: iv, 68, 77, 99
    rights abuses: 128
    spirit: 32, 83
    values: 184
humanity: 82, 84, 159, 162, 163, 174
    faith in: 99
    history of: 88
    hope for: 165
    lack of: 29
    suffering of: 80
humanity's time on Earth: 27
humankind: 1, 57-8, 174
humility: 109
Hunger Games, The: 179
hunger: 29, 162
hunter-gatherers: 6, 66
Huxley, Aldous: 49-50

Hyper-Anthropocene age: 175
hyperinflation: 18
idealism of the sixties: 34
ideology: 151, 153
Il-sung, Kim: 74
immediate gratification: 111
immigrants: 69
impersonal:
    arrangements: 15
    communism: 71-2, 76, 79
incentive structure: 7, 37
incentive-caused bias: 7
incentives: 14, 73, 112, 117, 135
income: 6, 28, 44, 73, 94, 98, 134, 139, 156
    source of: 21
    and wealth inequality: 134
India: 2, 25, 32, 148
Indiegogo: 96
indigenous cultures: 34
individual:
    expression: 104
    judgment: 58
    wealth: 108
individuality: 104
individuals: 44, 69, 142, 183
indolence: 80
indulgence: 28
industrial:
    chemicals: 122
    progress: 27
    revolution: 80
    workers: 81
industrialist leaders: 103
industrialization: 79, 152

selfless service: 115, 154
selflessness: 83
selling loose cigarettes: 55
sensitivity to popular will: 146
sensitivity: 6, 53, 128
sensual pleasures: 111
serenity: 109
serfs: 23, 26
service industries: 92
services:
   ecosystem: 120
   financial: 51
   goods and: 20, 63, 78, 82, 91, 101-2, 152, 161
   legal and prison: 101
   products and: 44, 63
   social: 107
sexual attraction: 39
shame: 40, 114, 125
   remorse and: 127, 128
shared:
   culture: 139
   experience: 145
shareholders: 46, 155
sharks: 66
shellfish: 120
shelter: 81, 94, 135, 154
ships: 87
shock point: 13
shopping: 104
Siberia: 60, 152
sickness: 81, 107
simplicity: 96, 112, 127
sincerity: 109
Singapore: 129-30

single-party rule: 152
Skype: 87
slaughterhouse: 181
slavery: 50
slaves: 47
small print: 54
Smith, Adam: 44-5
Snowden, David: 156
soap operas: 28
sociability: 67
social:
   collapse: 171-2
   context: 8
   convention: 36
   Darwinists: 70
   interaction: 67
   justice: 43
   media: 67, 93, 145
   networks: 66, 89
   progress: 70
   propriety: 39
   relationships: 14, 65
   responsibility: 45-6
   safety nets: 25
   services: 107
   -technical systems: 90
socialism: 61, 63, 152
soil: 26, 47, 122, 164-5
   degradation: 26, 164
   erosion: 122
Solar System: 11
solidarity: 60, 184
solitary confinement: 182
solitude: 60
solvency: 16, 44

Made in the USA
Middletown, DE
02 February 2016